Jenny
resour
Charte
Psycho
line, a
develo
counse
Diplor
Institu
counse
skills
advise

selling skills and approaches into their people development programmes.

Lyn van Oudtshoorn is an independent consultant/counsellor based
in Oxford. Her specialist field is organisational issues in workplace
counselling, with an emphasis on strategy and setting up best practice. She has worked one-to-one at all levels in organisations – counselling, coaching, and mentoring – and is also an experienced Relate
counsellor. Her groundbreaking research on integrating counselling
into organisation culture, *The Organisation as a Nurturing
Environment* (1989, MA thesis), is still widely quoted. She is currently completing a PhD research project on counselling as a
Learning Conversation with the Centre for the Study of Human
Learning at Brunel Univ

D0268599

developing practice

Other titles in the series:

The Institute of Personnel and Development is the leading publisher of books and reports for personnel and training professionals and students and for all those concerned with the effective management and development of people at work. For full details of all our titles please telephone the Publishing Department on 0181 263 3387.

COUNSELLING IN THE WORKPLACE

**Jenny Summerfield and
Lyn van Oudtshoorn**

INSTITUTE OF PERSONNEL AND DEVELOPMENT

© Jenny Summerfield and Lyn van Oudtshoorn 1995

First published in 1995

Typeset by The Comp-Room Aylesbury
Printed in Great Britain by The Cromwell Press, Wiltshire

British Library Cataloguing-in-Publication Data
A catalogue record for this book is available from the British Library

ISBN 0-85292-580-8

The views expressed in this book are the authors' own, and may not necessarily reflect those of the IPD.

INSTITUTE OF PERSONNEL
AND DEVELOPMENT

IPD House, Camp Road, London SW19 4UX
Tel: 0181 971 9000   Fax: 0181 263 3333
Registered office as above. Registered Charity No. 1038333
A company limited by guarantee. Registered in England No. 2931892

CONTENTS

ACKNOWLEDGEMENTS

We are grateful to many people who have helped us write this book. They have supported us with both practical help and encouragement. In particular we thank Roger Harrison, Carolyn Highley, Noreen Tehrani, Cathy Carroll and Lorren Wyatt for providing us with valuable insights and research. Colleagues at Interactive Skills have tip-toed around us and not complained when we hogged the word processors, printers and photocopier. We owe a debt to the many clients, companies and individuals, who have shared their personal experiences of counselling with us.

Most importantly, we would like to thank our family and friends; Chris, Maisie, Steve, Wendy, Heather and children Luke and Tanja for sharing their time with us and giving us endless moral support.

INTRODUCTION

It occurred to us, one day over a shared meal and a meeting of minds, that though there are countless books on counselling, only a tiny handful concern themselves with the workplace. Those that do, approach the organisation from a counselling point of view. We could not think of one that approached counselling from an organisational point of view. There certainly was not a single book we could recommend to human resource professionals that would answer the kind of questions we were both continually being asked. We would have to write it ourselves, we decided. Here it is.

We have written it for management as well as human resource professionals who would like to know more about what counselling has to offer in the workplace. We have not written the book for counsellors, though we hope that professional counsellors looking for a window on the organisational world will find material here that is of interest.

The book is presented in three parts to cover three distinct areas: Part One is about strategic issues for counselling in the workplace. It explores the kinds of questions organisations should ask when they decide to set up a counselling service, eg whether to contract in or out. It is vital, we believe, that counselling is not superimposed upon the organisation culture, but integrated into it. Counselling, whether directly delivered one on one or in the form of training and skills development, needs to be a process that dovetails into an organisation's mission, people, culture and its language. We suggest the practicalities of how HR and line managers can balance their job roles with their involvement in counselling. We present the view that a more carefully measured and structured approach at the beginning creates a more effective and responsive finished product.

Part Two looks at the counselling process itself, very briefly outlining some of the models that we have found useful in the workplace context. We also discuss some of the commonest issues of workplace counselling from both personal and organisational perspectives. In drawing this distinction we are very well aware that it is an artificial one. However hard we may try not to, we all take home to work with us, and then we bring work home. What affects one area of our lives inevitably affects the whole. We offer suggestions to help human resource professionals and line managers give appropriate support in dealing with these issues, and suggest cut-off points for referral to appropriate people or agencies.

Part Three addresses the question of training. We walk the reader through counselling skills training and compare it with full professional counsellor training. We make suggestions and offer guidelines for both the design and delivery of courses. This is training in its traditionally accepted sense. We also look at training in the broader developmental sense of the word. This encompasses the use of counselling skills and approaches in coaching, mentoring and performance management. We see counselling skills as the 'liquid engineering' of people management, oiling the wheels of good management practice. In Chapter 11 we consider the contribution it can make towards the long-term success of empowerment and change management programmes. Viewed in this light, embedding counselling skills into an organisation's culture can be seen as not only an act of generosity but also as an exercise in enlightened self-interest.

Worried sick, or 'worried well'?

The word *counselling*, in itself, has always been a difficult one in organisational cultures. We toyed briefly with the idea of calling it something else because we suspect that that is exactly the reason the term 'employee assistance programme' has gained such wide acceptance. But we came down on the side of the single word because that is what we are talking about. The problem is not the word itself, but the idea that underpins it. It is associated in many minds with the deficit or 'sickness' approach to well-being. The idea needs to shift to a positive, learning model.

Counselling is about problem-solving and improving working

relationships, not sickness. It refers not only to what is going wrong, but also what could be going better . . .

> It has often been said that we use only a fraction of our human potential; therefore, we should be capable of dealing much more creatively with ourselves, our relationships with others, and with the social settings of our lives. Counsellors can help their clients empower themselves by encouraging them to identify and develop unused or underused opportunities and potential.[1]

We believe that the time has come for a new vision. This new vision is one in which the enormous potential for an integrated, learning approach to counselling is embraced, creating growth not only for individual employees but for the organisation as a whole.

References

1. EGAN G. (1986). *The Skilled Helper*. Andover, Brooks Cole, p. 3.

PART 1

COUNSELLING: STRATEGIC APPROACHES

1

WHY COUNSELLING AT WORK?

It seems a very short while ago that the notion of counselling was regarded as having no place in commercial organisations. The word itself was anathema, and the function – when it was allowed at all – was relegated to a far-flung corner of the system, the building and the corporate psyche.

Now it is a hot topic. In some companies the word has been heard in the highest circles and in many it is even established. The bandwagon has begun to roll. Nowadays the danger lies less in denying the need than in being so confused by choice that discriminating quality from the gloss becomes very difficult.

From being a symbol of sickness, counselling has become a symbol of an organisation that is taking care of its health. What has created this change of heart? A number of influences, both internal and external, have combined to push counselling higher up the organisational agenda and the process of change is right at the top of the list. The Confederation of British Industry is giving counselling a higher profile, reporting in a comprehensive study that 'there is a need for organisations to take an integrated approach to employee well-being and to develop integrated employee wellness policies and procedures'.[1] Much has been said on the subject of employee well-being and, whilst we do not deny that this is a vital issue, we also see this as only one side of the coin where the usefulness of counselling is concerned.

Programmes embedding counselling skills and approaches into good management practice affect the bottom line favourably. Such programmes are measurable financially in tangible ways, for example, by reducing absenteeism and making a positive inroad into the 40 million working days lost in the UK every year owing to stress and mental illness.

The time has come for a new relationship between organisations and their employees, one that will regain the commitment and enthusiasm so sorely needed following the ravages of our much publicised recession.

Many organisations are searching for ways to regain commitment and have turned to new concepts, some of which are very useful but have somehow fallen short of expectations. With many of these management systems, the 'engine' is sound but the 'oil' is missing. We believe that the oil is the creating of new working relationships based on counselling skills and approaches – based on trust, respect and mutual understanding. Human resource managers have a vital role to play in helping to bridge the worlds of counselling, management and employees, for the mutual benefit of all.

Our view is that organisations deserve to be successful and that the human beings that work for them deserve both mental and emotional well-being.

Let us look in more detail at both the positive reasons and some of the trip-wires that exist, which suggest why counselling should be high on the organisational agenda.

What will organisations gain?

The following examples represent a more organisationally focused counselling strategy. They demonstrate:

□ creating feedback loops back up into higher management levels so that the organisation can benefit from the insights gained

□ embedding counselling/communication skills into management development

□ addressing real organisational issues as well as personal issues.

Knowledge is power How do organisations get a look in the mirror at themselves? Flawed management practices and business policies filter down and settle like mud at the grass roots of an organisation, choking its growth at an individual human level. An internal company counsellor who is down there on the ground, knowing exactly what is going on in the organisation, has a wealth of insight to offer its leaders.

One internally based counsellor whom we spoke to works for a huge public-sector organisation and represents the counselling function at board level. She advises not only on current issues affecting productivity but also on the likely impact of strategy on human resources whilst business plans are still at the discussion stage.

Releasing knowledge and enhancing creativity Some organisations, especially in the USA, have created 'knowledge cultures' that have dramatically increased business success. One company achieved this by breaking down the barriers between managers and employees and creating mutual trust and respect. New working relationships were formed. In the general enthusiasm that followed these moves new knowledge was released into the business that employees had previously no channel for sharing. People's capabilities and experience were being underused – they had much more knowledge than the organisation was tapping into. Creativity was enhanced and the ongoing financial success of the organisation is still enviable.

It's lonely at the top Counselling can provide feedback on sensitive issues on an individual basis.

An organisational counsellor, being on neutral ground, was able to tackle a company director about his over-controlling management style. No one wanted to risk the wrath of this director and he was steadily losing all of the talent from his team of managers. Productivity was falling in his department, and absenteeism rising. The human resources director had, fortunately, set up an executive coaching programme to include managers at the highest level. It was as part of this performance management programme that the counsellor, acting on information from the HR director, was able to tackle this thorny issue and suggest some different management approaches. An interesting point is that the director honestly believed that his style was acceptable because no one had told him otherwise.

Trip-wires

A combination of potentially problematic internal and external issues may draw organisations towards counselling. These include:

- □ uncertainty about litigation; industrial tribunals and stress claims
- □ poor performance counselling systems; individual and group performance
- □ 'presenteeism'; here in body but not in spirit.

The following examples illustrate how counselling can help organisations avoid some of these trip-wires.

Avoiding litigation: the case of Theresa A valued employee for eight years, Theresa was a high-flyer, but had been over-promoted. Mistakes had become unacceptably frequent, and their severity was potentially damaging for the company and the morale of her team. Theresa's manager had no idea how to deal with this. He had no counselling skills training and had no idea how to approach her. Conversations resulted in arguments and arguments resulted in the company taking disciplinary procedures. It was at this point that her husband, a powerful industrialist, stepped in and threatened to take legal action. Out of desperation the company called in a counsellor to try to sort Theresa out.

Within the non-threatening frame of the counselling relationship Theresa first began to unload some of the enormous stress (and distress) that had dogged her, and then to start to make sense of what was happening to her. Issues about lack of training and inept management arose, but Theresa blamed herself and so did her company; it was simply the easy way out to get rid of her. Theresa was emotionally locked into the 'victim' role.

So how did the counselling help? When the time came for her second disciplinary hearing she stunned everyone by her logical and clear approach to her own defence and, a little later, she stunned even her counsellor by announcing that she had decided to market herself internally and had obtained a new job, in a different department at a lower grade. Clearly the counselling had increased Theresa's ability to think rationally and evaluate her own skills and ability, and given her the confidence to act. The company had avoided a possible messy legal case by reaching an honourable solution. Everyone could save face.

Litigation and stress A case that hit the headlines this year was that of Walker *v.* Northumberland County Council, cited as the first case in the UK where an employee has sued his employer for stress-related illness and won. Amidst all the media coverage and 'hype' about this case organisations may be concerned about the wave of stress claims predicted by lawyers. Although we deal with counselling and the law in more detail later in this book, we need to say here that what many overlook is the fact that the Walker case has some unique features. Suing an organisation for stress-related illness is not as clear-cut as some are implying. Nevertheless, if the UK follows the USA on this there will be more litigation.

A more constructive approach to the whole subject would be to see the main benefit in the prevention of stress as greater employee health and well-being, reduced absenteeism and greater productivity, rather than the avoidance of litigation.

Poor performance counselling systems: the case of Andrew The organisation concerned did not consider that it needed career development strategies to manage high-flyers. Their way of handling them was to offer promotion. When Andrew, technically brilliant and academically talented, outgrew both the rewards and excitement of his job, the organisation duly promoted him to management. Andrew became unhappy and sought out the internal company counsellor.

Appraisals had been poor and, for someone so accustomed to success, the first taste of failure was a devastating blow. He told the counsellor that he needed to sort out his image problem but, after a while, the real reasons for his failure became clear. He never wanted to be a manager, he had no idea how to handle people, but he felt that he *ought* to know, and so did his manager, friends and partner at home.

The counsellor helped Andrew to set aside other people's views and decide what *he* really wanted. It may not have been mere coincidence that the counsellor reports having seen five other managers in the organisation with the same problem.

There are, of course, issues about training and assessment in this example. However, the organisation did not recognise the basic need for performance counselling, nor did it train its managers or human resource professionals in the counselling skills needed to do the job. In flatter structures with fewer promotion prospects, counselling in performance management becomes vital. When there are fewer jobs, talented people may stay where they are – even when they are over-promoted or not suited to management. As the recession lifts and more opportunities become available, attrition is a real danger. Organisations may miss a vital opportunity to retain good people, by blocking or ignoring valuable sources of feedback on their policies and practices.

When the problem is a whole department: The case of Carl
Carl was a member of a group who were at the end of the production line with responsibility for packaging, monitoring and dispatching lethal chemical substances, as well as safely disposing of contaminated material. It was a dirty and difficult job. When Carl was perceived to be displaying uncooperative behaviour, the company tried to get rid of him by offering a severance package; however, he did not want to go and involved his union, which supported him.

A counsellor was called in to see if Carl's attitude could be improved. The human resources manager admitted privately to the counsellor that his department was the company repository for 'no-hopers' and was unofficially seen as 'the department of the dead and the dying'. Acting within the boundaries of confidentiality the counsellor built up Carl's trust enough to hear his story.

Significantly, he was by now the only one left in the department. Two had left the organisation and one had asked to be moved to another department. Quite separately from the issue of poor management (conflicting orders from the supervisor and her line manager), it was clear that the whole group knew how they were labelled and lived up (or rather down) to it. Being undervalued, they acted out the role of 'no-hopers' and Carl's behaviour could have been seen as sabotage or as a cry for recognition.

We will never know what ideas people in the department may have had to improve productivity and add value or, on a more mundane level, how hard and well they may have worked if the organisation had openly recognised and valued the critical nature of their work.

This example goes beyond teambuilding and into the realms of working relationships involving respect and trust. Furthermore, it was a situation where a systems approach to the whole problem could have made a significant positive impact, had it been referred to a counsellor earlier.

Presenteeism: here in body but not in spirit We could say that organisations have been through sweeping changes: downsizing, privatisation, mergers, affecting not only those who have lost their jobs, but the 'survivors' who report cynicism, insecurity and disorientation that they are experiencing in the aftermath. One troubled employee of a large engineering organisation reported to a counsellor, 'We all arrive an hour earlier and leave two hours later because we are afraid that we will be next on the redundancy list. There is a lot more work than before, but we just do the minimum in order to survive.'

The case for counselling in the workplace
Through the real examples in this first chapter we have explored the more conventional way of using counselling resources in industry, ie for the resolution of employees' problems. We have also presented our conviction that counselling in the workplace has far more than this to contribute: a contribution that can improve the business performance of organisations. In the following chapters we aim to provide human resources and line managers with the starting points within counselling skills and approaches that will add value to the bottom line.

References

1.   WALDEGRAVE W. (1992). 'Introduction', in R. Jenkins and N. Coney, *Prevention of Mental Ill-health at Work*. London, HMSO for the CBI and Department of Employment, pp. ix–xiv.

2

ORGANISATIONAL PERSPECTIVES

Shaping an organisation counselling strategy that is both meaningful to the individual and relevant to the organisation is a process of careful planning.

There are four elements to the process:

□ The needs analysis – this involves asking the right questions and setting objectives. In this way, the *real* counselling needs of both individual and organisation can be accurately targeted.

□ Options – looking critically at all of the possibilities, making a choice, and designing a suitable programme

□ Setting up quality checks and measures

□ Formulating a policy for sound practice.

If an organisation sets up counselling provision without first knowing exactly what its needs and purposes are, then it will never know whether they are being met. This may sound like a statement of the obvious. However, recent research at UMIST[1] reveals that external employee assistance programmes are frequently purchased without a clear idea of the options available, and without adequate – if any – assessment of the organisation's precise needs. These two omissions are then almost always (in the UK) compounded by a third – that once an external EAP has been set in place, there is no monitoring of quality and therefore very few changes are made.

Organisations have not quite known where to put this stranger in their midst. A growing number recognise its value. Yet how to position the counselling function, where and how to link it into other organisation processes, whilst maintaining its independence, is still unclear to many. Not knowing how to position counselling, many organisations have placed it 'outside'. From there, it is unable to reach or address many of the issues we raise in this book.

Organisations are infinitely diverse, and therefore no solution is universal. Culture, cost, logistics, objectives . . . so many factors come into play when weighing up choices and needs, that it must be very tempting when faced with the promise of a 'one-stop solution' to look no further. It is critical, however, that organisations do examine the options, because every subsequent decision hangs on that first vital decision – to contract in or out.

The first step along the road toward a coherent strategy is the needs analysis. What follows is a broad-brush outline of needs analysis in the context of organisation cultures.

Needs analysis

The objective is to provide a sufficient framework to help organisations decide whether to contract in or out. Once that decision is made, more specialised questions may be needed to help decide how to shape the system. The questions to consider are these:

1   Who or what has driven the initiative?
2   What do senior management want from the provision?
3   What does the human resource function want from the provision?
4   What do individual employees, including management, want from the provision *for themselves*?
5   For each of the above three interest-groups, what are the priorities?
6   What structures/support systems are already in place?
7   What are the logistical and economic constraints?
8   What level of quality assurance is required, and how will quality be monitored?
9   How will the programme be marketed?
10 How will the programme be evaluated?
11 How will the programme fit in with the organisation's culture?

These questions are offered as a prompt in looking at the relevant issues. If the questions raised here are thought through in a systematic way (as elaborated below), the answers should build up a profile from which it will be possible to frame a set of both qualitative and quantitative objectives. Clear objectives will, in turn, help to clarify choices from amongst the options available and at a later stage provide reference points against which effectiveness can be measured. The list is also not intended to be exhaustive; there may be more questions, but there should not be fewer.

1 Who or what has driven the initiative?

Is there a specific problem? For instance:

☐ a recurring problem among employees, such as bereavement
☐ a looming round of redundancies
☐ a consistently high-risk environment, such as the risk of violent assault?

If so, it might be possible to begin with a specialised counselling provision such as stress/outplacement/post-trauma, and carefully monitor the process for indications of the less conspicuous layers of need.

Is there a generalised, less easily defined problem? Eg:

☐ high stress levels (might become evident through suicides, absenteeism, marital breakdowns, etc.)
☐ falling quality of service (higher rate of complaints)
☐ falling performance levels (falling output)
☐ high levels of conflict between individuals, levels, within teams, etc.
☐ poor communication patterns?

(Both of the last two indicators might become apparent through levels of disciplinary problems, errors etc.)

Organisations will become aware of generalised problems in a more diffuse way. A stress indicator questionnaire might help to focus more clearly on the nature of the difficulty. Another way would be to pilot a programme that addresses the general area – eg a general counselling provision, a stress management programme, a performance counselling programme, etc. – and then to use feedback from the programme as a diagnostic tool to locate the stressors. In this way the provision can be built more gradually and in direct response to need.

2 What do senior management want from the provision?
– In what specific ways will the programme line up with the organisation mission?
– Are board or senior management levels committed to the success of the programme?
 The more top-level support the programme has, the more strategically effective it is able to be.

3 What does the human resource function want from the provision?
– What kind of support does the HR function need?
– Where and at what level will the programme fit in with other organisational processes?
 Even though the programme will need to be professionally independent (on the grounds of ethical and political sensitivity, and also of confidentiality – see Chapter 3) it will still need a network along which lines of referral, communication and responsibility may be channelled. This will be true also for external programmes. Someone within the organisation will be first point of liaison, and someone will carry ultimate responsibility for its effectiveness. How will these links be established, and how will they be maintained, with whom, and why? The links need to be strong: if this communication network is not robust enough, the programme will become increasingly isolated and unable to function effectively.
 In thinking creatively around this issue of 'fit', it might be helpful to consider the way in which the total quality system operates, as a kind of parallel logic. The similarities are quite striking.

Total Quality Management	Integrated Counselling Function
• is a facilitating role	• is a facilitating role
• concerned with quality of practice – oils the wheels of practice	• concerned with quality of communication and morale – oils the wheels of communication
• must be seen as *independent* in order to avoid partiality and territorial sensitivities	• must be seen as *independent* in order to allay fears about confidentiality and avoid clouding professional judgement

• most important *interface* is with customer, therefore sits alongside manufacturing (usually)	• most important *interface* is with employee, therefore sits alongside human resources (usually)
• must provide a *network* of support systems, ensuring that all necessary questions are asked, and answered	• must provide a *network* of support systems, ensuring that all 'specialist' needs are met

Just as total quality programmes are now seen to be necessary and have been effectively integrated into existing structures and systems, so the counselling function will become a hall-mark of a healthy workplace.

4 What do individual employees, including management, want from the programme for themselves?

– A well-designed questionnaire will not only help to target the most pressing areas of concern without wasting resources, it will also serve greatly to enhance trust in the programme when it is in place.

5 For each of the above three interest groups (senior management, human resources and individual employees), what are the priorities?

– Is there a correlation?

It may be possible to accommodate all primary concerns in one system, but the likelihood is that some combination of options will be more acceptable if the programme is to have a broad relevance.

6 What structures/support systems are already in place?

– How effective are they?

– Where are the gaps?

It may be that all that is required is to add on to existing resources and to provide effective management of that net-work. This would depend on the effectiveness of what is already in place, and the degree of shortfall in other areas. Add-ons may make the whole network too unwieldy, though, and in many cases it may be simpler and more effective in the longer term to start from scratch. It is important to have a coherent system not only for manageability but also for accessibility. Ease of entry for potential users into the helping system must be a priority.

7 *What are the logistical and economic constraints?*

– Is the organisation a single or multisite operation? What is the total number of employees and how are they distributed among sites? How far are the sites geographically spread?
– What financial resources are available, and how can these be used to maximum benefit?

If the sites are sufficiently close or if different sites are large enough, this may not be an issue in terms of cost. These questions are discussed more fully on page 32.

8 *What level of quality assurance is required, and how will quality be monitored?*

Selection, training, professional supervision and programme management are all areas to be considered in ensuring quality. Independent benchmarking quality audits are not yet, but will become, important exercises for external programmes, as user organisations become more discriminating in matters of quality.

9 *How will the programme be marketed?*

However well-designed and well-run the programme is, it will not be used unless it is effectively marketed within the organisation. All levels of employees need to know that the programme is there, what it is for and how to access it. They must know that their confidentiality will be protected. Managers need to learn how to use the programme to facilitate their work (though not as an alternative to good management!) and how and when to refer to the programme. Organisations that decide to implement referral-only rather than open-access programmes will need to provide regular orientation sessions for managers. Marketing must take careful account of the cultural biases of the organisation; for example, status-conscious cultures may want to emphasise different levels of provision, or 'macho' cultures will offer help in much less obvious language. Each organisation will know best what is or is not acceptable in its own environment. Lastly, the marketing must be ongoing. Statistics reveal that after marketing exercises there is invariably a surge in take-up, which subsides again over time.

10 How will the programme be evaluated?

Evaluation is important to most organisations, but hard data is difficult to come by in counselling and training evaluation. This may be one reason the benefits have been slow in gaining recognition. If needs are carefully analysed and objectives clearly set, some measures can be taken. Subjective data should not be ignored, however, because in this field it is as valid as hard data in measuring results. This is explored further in the final section of this chapter.

11 How will the programme fit with the organisation's culture?

This question is really an extension of question two. If the *mission* is an expression of the organisation's declared aims and values, then the *culture* is what actually happens in practice. The unconscious motives of the organisation will also be reflected in its policies and prevailing style of management, and therefore the counselling style it adopts – or indeed whether it adopts one at all – makes a real statement about its culture and its value-system. The programme may be a precursor to, or a part of, culture change, but it will still need to be sensitive to the existing culture in order to get alongside the employees it seeks to serve.[2]

The culture of an organisation is often taken for granted from within, but some appreciation of the demands of particular cultures will be helpful in formulating objectives.

The cultural context

There are some organisations that will readily embrace counselling as a part of their cultural ethos. There are others that will fight it to the last ditch. Ironically, this can work in inverse proportion to need – the 'hardest' cultures that make the heaviest demands are often the least amenable to the idea of providing support.

Organisational consultant Roger Harrison has identified four fundamental organisation styles, which he calls archetypes. His Model of Organisation Culture[3] can be used as a framework for understanding the relationship between organisational style and counselling style.

Many of the needs arising may be common to the different organisational cultures because people bring their same inner conflicts to work in whatever organisation culture they find themselves. However, different issues are provoked in the different cultures, and they can be expected to trigger somewhat different reactions. Using his latest version of the model, the different issues posed by each of the cultures and the responses they are likely to provoke, are as follows:

The *transactional* culture 'at its best offers security in return for compliance. There is always a hidden threat of punishment or withdrawal of benefits behind even the most benevolent control, and therefore, these organizations can be said to run on fear, as well as hope of reward. At their worst, transactional organizations are despotic, tyrannous, and full of fear.'[4]

The particular counselling issues here are likely to centre around dependency or its mirror image, rebellion. Referrals may be made to counsellors with the intention of persuading employees to comply. Design of a counselling provision for this kind of organisation will therefore need to be especially careful about safeguarding the independence of counsellors.

In *self-expression* cultures, people tend to be driven by a desire to achieve. This culture offers them recognition and reward, as well as the opportunity to do exciting work. However, the constant striving for promotion and status means that people here suffer from the fear of failure. They will often exploit themselves in the pursuit of success, to the detriment of their health and well-being.

The burning issue for counsellors here will be stress, overload and burnout. There are also likely to be anxieties brought about by the lack of structure, competition and pressure to achieve. People in self-expression cultures need to adjust to the lack of support which is typical of the self-expression organisation, to become more autonomous, and to look to themselves rather than to authorities for resources. For this same reason also, it is possible that organisations in the true self-expression mould may be more sceptical than others about what counselling can offer.

Alignment cultures tend to be idealistic, and their employees committed. It differs from the self-expression type in that

the driving force is desire for excellence, rather than for grati-
fication. There is a single-minded dedication to the pursuit of
goals and purposes, the quality Tom Peters describes as a 'pas-
sion for excellence'. High demands are made on members'
energy and time, and counsellors will encounter conflicts in
those having to make difficult choices between commitment
to the organisation and outside ties to family, friends, community, and so on.

Mutuality cultures are those in which most value is placed
on connection, belonging and mutual support. Harrison
likens these organisations to high-performing sports teams, or
a jazz combo, in which the lead is passed back and forth
among the players, and the concept of the 'work' develops out
of the interaction among them. These are the environments
likely to have the least need for work-related counselling, and
where the core values (see Chapter 4, page 62) and skills will
be naturally in evidence. In a sense this is the 'ideal' culture,
which flows spontaneously from the values and communication skills we describe – whether it comes naturally, or is the
result of training.

As every organisation is an entirely unique system (there
is no pure type), it follows that no two will have exactly the
same needs. If counselling is to make a positive impact on
the culture and performance of an organisation, it needs to
grow out of, and respond effectively to, these special needs,
and to a clearly defined set of objectives based on those
needs. It is important, therefore, that flexibility is high on
the shopping-list. It is not necessary to settle for an off-the-
peg service that fits only where it touches. Furthermore,
that flexibility must be ongoing and responsive to change.
However thorough a needs analysis may be in the first
instance, circumstances do change, and needs will evolve
accordingly.

In organisations where counselling functions are already in
place, these criteria may still be used in order to assess their
relevance to the real issues. Once this groundwork is com-
pleted and the objectives are set, the choices may then be
examined in the light of their relevance to a particular organisation.

The options

There are three basic options – external, internal and a combination of both – though within those three categories, and especially in the last, there is a whole range of possibilities. (NB: the term EAP is often mistakenly used to mean 'external provider' in the UK. We use the term generically, to cover all types of employee assistance.)

External providers

Growth in this area has been dramatic in recent years, perhaps because buying an external service is easier initially than setting up an independent counselling function. This has not been the case in the USA, where internal providers have led the field in EAP development.

The typical external provider offers a package of services to the client company in return for an annual subscription fee, which is calculated on a *per capita* basis regardless of how many employees actually use the service. The cost is also dependent upon the range of services provided, for example, whether or not to include employees' families, how many hours a day coverage, and so on. The client organisation can then negotiate its own combination of services, balancing its perceived need against the funds available.

The provider then subcontracts out to freelance affiliates and, depending on the size of the contractor, individual operators may be assigned to just one account or to several. Counsellors are employed in this way in different locations to give multisite coverage. It is this method of operating that gives the external EAP one of its main advantages for organisations with small units dispersed over a wide geographical area. (Having said that, it would be hard to imagine an organisation more geographically dispersed than the Post Office, whose combination internal/external Occupational Health Service is one of the most widely respected.)

By definition, counsellors operating through the external system are never directly employed by the client organisation; indeed, they are 'twice removed', the contracting provider in effect operating as a middle-man who manages the function on the one hand and links into the client organisation on the other.

Most external providers offer the following core components: 1) marketing the service in-house, both directly to employees and through the management network; 2) actual provision of the counselling and (from some) advice to managers on dealing with specific employee difficulties; and 3) feedback in the form of statistical reports.

There are several strengths and weaknesses inherent in this (and other) approaches to employee counselling, and we will discuss the relative merits of each after the following section.

Internal EAP programmes

Development of the internally based facility has lagged behind the external EAP in the UK, and far behind internally based facilities in the USA. This is a pity, because potentially the in-house programme has a great deal to offer. It is also harder to pin down and describe because by its nature it takes on the form of its context, or host organisation. Thus one might find anything from a highly sophisticated 'package' of specialised services linked to a central co-ordinating function, to a small and completely informal function.

Formal or informal, the internal programme is always highly individual, though there are some common characteristics. The two most distinctive features are that counsellors are themselves employees of the organisation, and that they work exclusively for that organisation. They may be full- or part-time, long-term employees or short-term contract holders. They may even be professionally trained or skills-trained counsellors who primarily serve other functions. See Chapter 3 for more on balancing roles.

Usually they operate as an extension of another function – either human resources, welfare or wellness – through whom they link into the organisation. And rarely, but most effectively, they operate as an entirely independent, free-floating business that is answerable to board level. This kind of service would still need to be networked to the other functions for referral and communication purposes.

The way the function is positioned in the organisation and the level at which it links in, is critical in establishing the level at which it will eventually operate and be accepted. This has happened much too randomly in the past. In consequence counselling services – by whatever name they are known – have suffered from isolation or low level functioning which has in turn seriously limited their effectiveness and scope. (External operators have been more able to leap-frog this credibility gap by coming in from the outside, and this has been their major selling advantage.) This situation can be avoided by approaching the whole question of counselling provision with the same thoroughness as a business would consider any other investment of its resources.

Because in-house programmes are usually quite small they need people with broadly based skills. Actual counselling skills will ideally include an integrated approach to theory, and experience of systems approaches and short-term focused work. Working with complex relationship issues also demands a deeper understanding of psychodynamic influences, for example transference, even though their application in the organisation setting will be more superficial than in traditional therapeutic settings. (Transference is a term that refers to the inappropriate transfer of feelings from one person to another, usually unconsciously. See Chapter 4 – the section on psychodynamic counselling on page 83 – for a fuller explanation of transference.)

Other competencies will reflect the range of support activities such people might be required to fulfil. Employee and management orientation, counselling skills training, counselling supervision, formulating policy, consulting to management, research, resource development and budget administration are all among the multiplicity of roles that are the legitimate concerns of a fully in-house function. Clearly this requires a person with acute business sensitivity as well as interpersonal qualities, and people trained and competent in these skill combinations are still hard to find. Personal attitudes are vital too. Professional counsellors who are out of sympathy with the basic commercial ethos would do better to stay away from the organisational context, as it is unlikely they would be able to manage the subtle balance of loyalties that the role demands. We discuss recruitment criteria more fully later in this chapter.

There is still a crying need for professionally trained counsellors who are 'cross-bred' from a business background. It is hoped that, as more professionals fitting that profile emerge, the in-house movement will gain its rightful place in the growing workplace counselling field. It is only the counsellor who operates from within the system who can appreciate the culture and communication difficulties within the organisation and can provide feedback to the organisation on issues which impact on staff. This is the unique contribution of the in-house provider.

HR professionals, and managers too, have an important role to play in the provision of first-level support and referral, moving in and out of the role of temporary counsellor. Where the counselling function is fully integrated, professional internal counsellors, HR professionals and external specialists or specialist agencies can all complement one another in providing a multilayered support system.

Internal *vs* external provision – the debate

We have briefly outlined the differences between external and in-house models of workplace counselling, but before we move on to the third model – what we call the integrated model – it is necessary to weigh the advantages and disadvantages of both of the above. That is because we believe that by drawing on a well-planned combination of external and internal, the advantages of both can be maximised while the disadvantages can be minimised, or even eliminated completely.

Confidentiality

This is the first priority of any comparison, because confidentiality is quite rightly the focus of much concern and vulnerability when counselling enters the workplace. The subject of confidentiality is covered in Chapter 3. For the purposes of strategic planning, though, the important thing to remember is this: confidentiality has nothing to do with whether the programme is internal or external, and everything to do with the individual person-to-person contract. A commitment to confidentiality needs to be made clear in the mission statement, in all orientation and publicity information, and then reinforced afresh at the point of entry for all users of the programme.

Confidentiality forms a fundamental part of professional training, and the professionalism of the counsellor is the only true basis of confidentiality. The only 'guarantee' therefore, is a rigorous system of quality checks that includes a well-defined recruitment and training policy, and professional supervision, and these can only be monitored effectively if the organisation takes ownership of the programme.

At an *inter*organisation level, the greater the number of accounts an external provider holds, the greater the potential risk of compromise on confidentiality for the organisation itself. Again, it is professionalism that holds sway. Disabuse your organisation of the notion that the only 'safe' counsellor is the one who is somewhere else . . . Real confidentiality rests on the quality of *individual* practitioners.

Independence and interface

Overlapping the question of confidentiality is another area, relating to the whole question of independence – perceived or real – and feedback.

It is our common experience in working with individuals in organisations that woven into personal issues are very often contextual issues. This means two things: first, there will be times when a counsellor needs to work in tandem with others – either HR or line – in the resolution of a particular problem. Secondly, it means that counsellors will often be first to become aware of something going wrong within the system. It is *vital* that this learning is not lost to the organisation, but that it is fed back in at a level high enough actually to address the root causes. This in no way compromises confidentiality. It is, however, a matter of professional discretion to separate out the private concerns of clients from general organisation concerns which are relevant to the effective functioning of the whole.

Where does one draw the line between feedback and legitimate intervention in the workplace on the one hand and confidentiality on the other? How does one preserve the free hand of independence working from within an organisation, or access the organisational perspective working from the outside? We will look more closely at these questions in the following chapter, but for now the purpose is to look at what actually happens in practice.

In 1988, while researching an academic paper, we were told by the then largest external EAP operating in the UK, that they 'would not touch' the organisation beyond negotiating the original deal and supplying formal statistical data. Response to the argument for the need for closer co-operation with client organisations, was 'Good luck!' Attitudes have changed somewhat in the intervening time. The need for constructive communication with organisations is now more widely recognised, and many external providers have been forced to confront some of the difficult questions raised above, rather than avoid them, if they were to survive.

In this regard, in-house programmes will always have a hands-down advantage over external providers simply by virtue of where they operate. Inside practitioners with even a little nous will very quickly learn the organisational ropes – the culture and values, the mission, the policies and procedures, the weaknesses and strengths, the political intrigues, the tender egos. Every little nuance of corporate life is relevant in understanding the issues and problems of individual employees, and helping to resolve them.

The UMIST/HSE research found that external providers did not see experience of workplace counselling as essential in their selection of counsellors. It further reports that, 'Most providers, worryingly, do not give counsellors information about client companies, as a matter of course. This only happens if it is felt necessary, for some reason, to give this information to counsellors.'[5] This might be why so many of the external counsellors themselves feel uneasy about dealing with specifically work-based issues. The report finds that: 'In terms of the counsellors' feelings about their actual counselling, the two areas which seem to cause dissatisfaction are tackling problems and resolving work-related problems.'

We believe that letting loose on an organisation counsellors who have neither experience of business in general nor of the organisation culture and style in particular is potentially dangerous both to the organisation and to the individual clients themselves.

Quality

There are some other disturbing facts about quality that have been highlighted by this report. Particularly, there seem to be major discrepancies between the way resources are presented to client organisations by providers, and the way the counsellors themselves see the service they offer. The counsellors surveyed report that:

- eight out of 10 say they are concerned about the levels of qualifications and experience of some counsellors, and the dangers for the client when faced with an inexperienced counsellor. A significant number hold no formal counselling qualifications, and of those that do, many hold only a basic, non-accredited Certificate in Counselling. A large number were recruited with no interview at all.

- 50 per cent use their own premises for counselling, but these have never been inspected by the EAP providers they work for. This is despite the fact that it is stipulated in their contract that the provider will visit their premises before they carry out any EAP work.

- 45 per cent rate the amount of training they have received from providers as almost non-existent

- nine out of 10 comment on the differing standards of EAP providers with regard to selection procedures, level of feedback, supervision, and training

- eight out of 10 are concerned about the service the client is receiving, particularly in relation to certain EAP providers who are considered to be providing a 'poor service' for the client, the counsellor and the client organisation.

This also raises concerns about the quality of initial client assessments. If the first-line counsellors are not focused or informed enough, there is a possibility that however expert the available specialist services are, those in need might not be referred on appropriately. Given that, for instance, financial difficulty is just as potentially life-threatening as anorexia, and that both are areas of specialist concern, these are matters that deserve the most serious consideration.

To employ a service that will only tolerate self-evaluation is an extraordinary leap of faith, particularly considering what is at stake and what is actually happening. Yet independent audits are still not being taken seriously enough by organisations, and are being strenuously resisted by external providers.

There are only two routes to quality assurance. The first is for the organisation itself to set the standards and monitor quality, which is only possible with an in-house programme; or, for an external programme, to insist upon the right to use an independent audit. Either way, the issue of quality is one that is trailing behind in the development of EAPs, and one that needs to be urgently addressed.

The EAPA has done a sterling job of mapping out the standards of practice and professional guidelines for EAPs but in practice, unfortunately, most fall far short of the mark. The EAPA does not at present enforce these guidelines among its members (and it is difficult to see how they would do so without independent audits), and neither does it have the authority to prevent any outside group of people setting itself up as an EAP and operating a seriously substandard service. This would have to be a matter for legislation. In fairness, it must be said that the same is true of counselling in general, and that a very wide spectrum, ranging from amateurism to expertise, calls itself by that name, and that it is very difficult for anyone not knowing the system to tell the difference.

Recruitment criteria for counsellors must take four things into account:

□ the quality of training. Accreditation by a recognised body, such as The British Psychological Society, British Association for Counselling, or Relate, guarantees a certain standard of training and experience. It does not, however, automatically exclude counsellors operating outside the 'system'. Some very fine counsellors do.

□ the depth of experience ... and, where specialist skills are required, the *direct* experience in working with that specific problem – eg drug abuse, post-trauma stress, etc. (See Matrix in Chapter 4.) Experience of short-term work is also crucial.

- ☐ the theoretical orientation of the counsellor (see Chapter 4 for a fuller explanation) and, very importantly,

- ☐ the values and personal qualities of the counsellor. Beware of counsellors who hold an anti-organisation view. Counsellors operating in this field *must* be sympathetic to it, and should be 'bilingual' – ie able to speak the language of the commercial world as well as the language of counselling. Without this 'street cred', their capacity to function across the culture divide will be minimal.

Logistics, cost and specialism

Many organisations employing external contractors have done so because of their need for multisite cover, and where an organisation is relatively small *and* very widely dispersed this is both a strategically and economically sound rationale.

The wide range of specialisms required is another reason often quoted for looking outside the organisation, and again this is a good reason – but not always. Specialist resources can be networked in a number of ways. Large organisations, because of sheer scale, can justify employing specialist advisers and counsellors either on a contract or consultancy basis. Small organisations can make use of advisory services in the community – Citizens Advice Bureaux, for instance, are hard to beat in terms of expertise. Dispersed organisations can contract in mobile units, and so on.

There is a kind of threshold effect operating between size in relation to spread and cost, and that is largely because of the diversity of specialist skills required. As a general rule of thumb, it is reasonable to work on the basis of one full-time counsellor per 3,500 employees. That is a straightforward calculation, and of course the much smaller organisation can employ an internal person on a part-time or even *ad hoc* basis. But the economic point of diminishing returns for external providers is much more difficult to pin down. For one thing, there are a great many variables – range of services required, differences between providers and so on – and, for another, the providers are not at all forthcoming about relative cost benefit. That is a piece of research the client organisation needs to carry out for itself. In the survey we have been quoting from,

23 internal counselling services were providing 618,000 employees with counselling, whereas the 122 external counselling services (including EAPs) were providing counselling to a total of only 197,000 employees. There would therefore appear to be a clear-cut case for the economic advantage of internal services.

Flexibility

This is the final point of comparison to consider between external and internal services, and one that takes us nicely onto the next section because the integrated, or combined, model is the ultimately flexible and responsive one.

Flexibility in the external variety of counselling consists in choosing from a range of service options, and then renegotiating them at the point of renewal. In practice it very seldom happens that any changes are made once the original package has been bought, and a survey of opinion suggests this has more to do with inertia than with customer satisfaction. Both in this and in terms of individual client benefit, flexibility is very limited.

Though short-term, focused work is more appropriate in the workplace, and in-house counsellors are aware of this too, there will always be valid exceptions to this principle. The in-house provider has much more scope for professional judgement in this regard as well as in regard to the special needs of the organisation. External providers have to exercise much more control over the number of sessions available to any one client, whether or not it is in the client's best interests to continue. This is because EAP contractors are just as concerned with unit costs and bottom-line profits as their client organisations.

The limits to flexibility of totally in-house systems (in small organisations) consist in the narrower range of skills represented by a smaller number of people, as we have already discussed in the previous section.

The integrated or combined model

This model, as the name suggests, uses elements of the internal and external models in varying combinations, but the system as a whole is embedded in and managed by the organisation itself. Taking this stance enables the organisation to use full discretionary power in creating a support function that exactly fits its needs, whilst at the same time employing the benefits and avoiding the disadvantages of each.

The provision can, for instance, be layered: a network of line and HR managers might provide first-stage help,

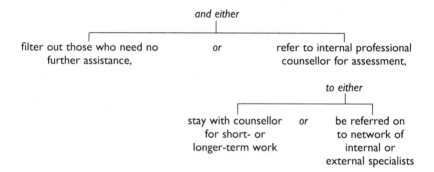

and either

filter out those who need no   *or*   refer to internal professional
further assistance,   counsellor for assessment,

to either

stay with counsellor   *or*   be referred on
for short- or   to network of
longer-term work   internal or
                                              external specialists

It can be hierarchically layered too, with either internal or consultant counsellors providing time off-site for senior management, external specialists employed *ad hoc* for all levels, and an in-house person providing assessment and general counselling.

Small organisations can contract-in on a part-time or even *ad hoc* basis. Large organisations can do so in a much more structured way. In a variety of ways the integrated model provides a solution to the problem of the size/cost-effectiveness threshold.

Ways of helping other than counselling *per se* can also be used to augment the system: for instance, education and training, seminars and workshops, etc. The permutations can be shaped in as many ways as there are organisations.

One thing remains constant, however, and that is the need for a powerfully cohesive force that takes responsibility for integrating and managing this network and making sure it is addressing the objectives. That person may be a company-employed specialist/manager; he or she may be a contracted-in consultant, who takes responsibility with a company inter-face person. The function of this person or this team would be to drive policy, ensure high quality, give feedback, provide or supply professional supervision, integrate the specialist network and keep the in-company referral network well oiled. In the case of the small organisation this person may also be the generalist counsellor, interfacing with the company link person on the one hand, and with external specialists on the other.

There is no mystique about what the external EAP function does. It is simply that role of managing networks of providers, but outside of the organisation's culture and out of range of its quality assurance systems.

We have discussed at length the range of possibilities available to organisations looking to set up a counselling function. In the two Figures that follow, we can see how two companies have responded creatively but differently to the challenges posed by their particular cultures.

Two working models

The Post Office

Size: 200,000 employees, dispersed over a wide geographical area. The care-function has grown and evolved in an 'organic' way. It takes varying forms, including educational programmes and training. The whole employee care framework consists of three separate, yet interdependent functions. In each function there are people with counselling skills, who are layered in terms of competency levels and areas of responsibility. Each level is regarded as an important aspect of the integrated whole. In recent years the care function has focused increasingly on the effects of violence at work, adopting an integrated response (see Chapter 6). The three functions are:

□ Occupational Health, which encompasses physical and mental health, including the counselling network

□ Welfare Services, which encompasses 'social well-being' and offers specialist advisory/support networks, and

□ Personnel, which covers aspects relating to organisational/ employee issues.[6]

Figure 1
THE POST OFFICE MODEL

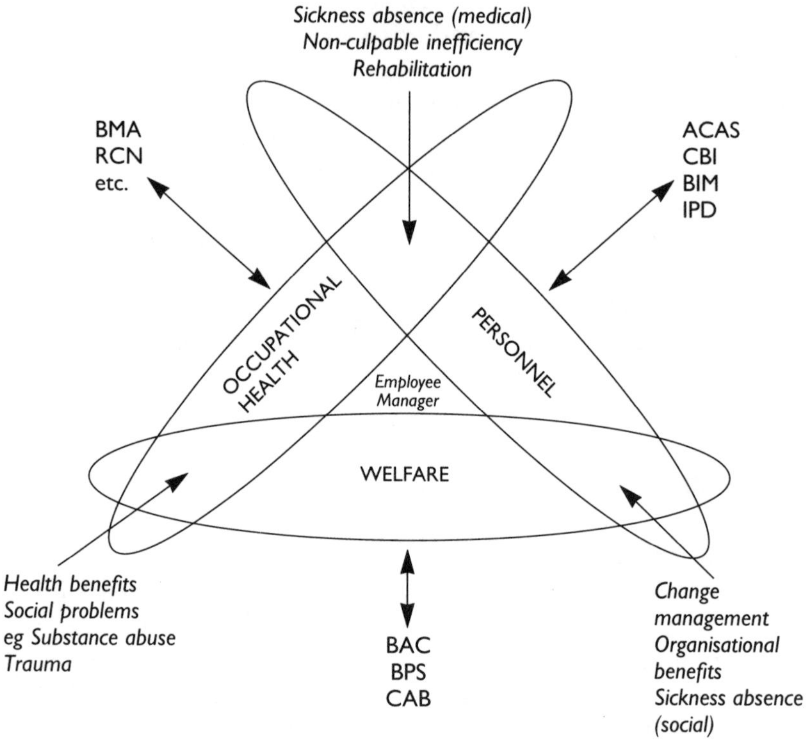

Sickness absence (medical)
Non-culpable inefficiency
Rehabilitation

BMA
RCN
etc.

ACAS
CBI
BIM
IPD

OCCUPATIONAL
HEALTH

PERSONNEL

Employee
Manager

WELFARE

Health benefits
Social problems
eg Substance abuse
Trauma

Change
management
Organisational
benefits
Sickness absence
(social)

BAC
BPS
CAB

Organisation 'B'

This is a media company employing 1,500 people on one site. The company has one internal counsellor who works solely for them, three days a week. She reports directly to the human resources director, and works in tandem with six HR managers who do first-level counselling, and refer deeper-level work to her. She in turn refers out of the organisation, when necessary, to a network of specialist advisers she has set up to provide services on an *ad hoc* basis.

Figure 2

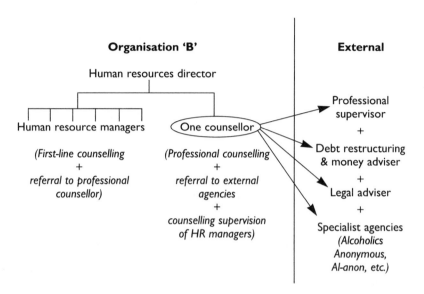

Auditing and evaluation

These two subjects are often confused, perhaps because the word 'audit' is commonly used as an accounting term. To clarify, *auditing* refers to the checking of quality, looking at issues of selection and qualification, training, supervision etc. and setting them against benchmarks. *Evaluation* is about the measurement of outcomes: cost benefit (in quantitative terms), and cost-effectiveness (in terms of more qualitative outcomes, such as well-being).

We have already covered the issue of quality at some length. In internal programmes quality can be monitored by the company itself, using its own quality guidelines; or, if it is considered desirable, outside audits can provide a fresh perspective and reassurance that all is well. We do not find an ethical problem with self-audit where the company is ultimately responsible for its own programme of care. In external EAPs, however, this does create an ethical problem because, in principle, having retained the EAP, the client company remains accountable for its employees if the care provision fails. How then can it afford to leave quality checks to the providers? The research shows quite conclusively that self-audit by external EAPs is failing significantly. This leaves organisations very vulnerable to litigation and this, in bald terms, is why quality auditing is so critical.

There is another profoundly important reason, though: the cost of getting it wrong can be very high, not just in economic terms, but in human terms also. Organisations that subscribe to all the principles of valuing their human resource, investing in people etc. must take this responsibility for quality very seriously.

Evaluation

The Post Office excepted, most detailed evaluation studies of counselling in the workplace have been done in the USA. There, the financial and other benefits of stress-care are widely recognised and most of the Fortune 500 companies have employee counselling services in place.

In the past many organisations have been willing to take the value of employee counselling as an article of faith or on the basis of subjective evidence only. But increasingly, both in the USA and in the UK, organisations are beginning to demand harder data. The kinds of statistical data that can be measured and independently verified are sickness/absentee rates, accident rates (both in and out of work – these are excellent indicators of stress), medical retirement rates, disciplinary initiatives, customer complaints, productivity/output etc. Statistical data that record only such things as counselling through-put and problem ratios refer inwardly to the process, and not outwardly to organisation issues. (Problem ratios can be indicators, though they can also be deceiving, because a presenting problem is often only a symptom of another problem.) The key to measuring outcomes with any degree of accuracy is to establish a mean or benchmark before the programme begins, and then to take measurements against it at agreed points. These may then be related to the organisation's defined needs, to assess whether the short-, medium- and long- term objectives are being met.

Of course, all of these indicators are subject to other variables, and so the more different measures one takes, the more reliable and three-dimensional a picture one can build up.

This is quite a complicated statistical process and, depending on the internal resources available, is probably best done on a consultative basis.

Qualitative data are more subjective and therefore less verifiable. Self-report by the client (by means of questionnaire) can be supported by appraisal information, but only where this can be obtained without compromising confidentiality. Whether or not it is verified, it should not be discounted as a valid – and valuable – source of information, though it is probably more usefully regarded as feedback than as measurement. Analysis of qualitative data is one of the fastest-growing areas of research.

Soft skills, hard results

Inviting counselling skills into the organisation mainstream in the ways we describe, opens the door also to a new style of communicating and learning that has positive and far-reaching implications for the whole business.

Having designed the programme, it is time to formulate policy and guidelines for practice. This is the subject of the next chapter.

References

1. HIGHLEY J. C. and COOPER C. L. (1994). *An Assessment of UK EAPs and Workplace Counselling Programmes*. (A Health and Safety Executive-funded project.) The full report will be published as a book in 1996.
2. VAN OUDTSHOORN L. (1989). 'The Organisation as a Nurturing Environment: An integrated approach to counselling in the workplace.' (M.A. thesis, Antioch University.)
3. HARRISON R. (1994). *Humanizing Change: Matching interventions to organizational realities*. Clinton, Washington, Harrison Associates.
4. HARRISON R. (1994). 'A New Model of Organization Culture', a paper adapting material from *Humanizing Change*. Clinton, Washington, Harrison Associates.
5. *Ibid*. p. 6.
6. TEHRANI N. (1994). 'Business dimensions to organisational

counselling.' *Counselling Psychology Quarterly*. Vol. 17, No. 3, p. 11.

Further reading

TEHRANI N. (1994). 'An Integrated Response to Trauma in Three Post Office Businesses'. Paper presented to the IPD conference in Harrogate, October 1994, and to be published in *Work and Stress* journal.

TEHRANI N. (1994). 'Organisational Counselling: Legal and ethical issues'. Paper presented at the British Psychological Society Conference on Counselling Psychology in London, 1994.

EAP ASSOCIATION (1995). *UK Standards of Practice and Professional Guidelines for Employee Assistance Programmes*. London, EAPA.

3

SETTING UP SOUND PRACTICE

We have described in detail how it is largely the needs of the organisation that set the parameters for a counselling *strategy*. It is the needs of the individual, however, that will form the ethical framework around which counselling *policy* is built.

Sooner rather than later, anyone practising counselling skills – whether professionally or as part of a wider management function – is going to come up against ethical dilemmas. There are few absolute rules. On the whole, the best we can do is to understand the general principles, the possible implications of our actions, and make considered judgements in pursuit of the client's best interests.

Who is the client? For the professional counsellor questions like: 'Might this person harm himself/someone else? Am I competent to deal with this problem? Have I done as much as I can? Shall I refer on? Should I reach out and touch this person, or would that be inappropriate?' are all in a day's work. Within an organisation, which effectively becomes a third party to the transaction, these issues take on another dimension which does not apply to counselling outside of the workplace.

There are two main reasons for this. First, those practising counselling skills in organisations are not always fully trained and experienced counsellors. There is a profound difference between using counselling skills on the one hand and being a fully trained, experienced counsellor on the other. Forgetting this distinction and sailing off into waters too difficult to navigate is far more dangerous than offering no help at all.

Secondly, there is often a perceived conflict of values, vested interests and loyalties. Hard-nosed business and 'soft-skill' counselling make an uneasy marriage. Mention the

'C'-word to many business managers and you may observe an ill-concealed shifting in the chair. Mention business aims to many counsellors and reactions will often vary from mild suspicion to open hostility. Counselling ceases to be counselling if it doesn't take the individual seriously enough, and it ceases to be viable if it fails to take the organisation seriously enough.

Between the two is the 'narrow way' – that interface where the counsellor operates. This double-sided contract forms the basis of the apparent ambiguity that is so often, mistakenly, put forward by counsellors as a dilemma: who is the client – the individual, or the organisation? The answer, we suggest, is both. As we suggested in Chapter 1, they are opposite sides of the same coin. The primary alliance must of course remain with the individual client, and all of the organisations in our experience recognise this principle. Ultimately, the needs of the organisation and the individual are not antagonistic to one another.

FIGURE 3
BALANCING ROLES IN ORGANISATIONS

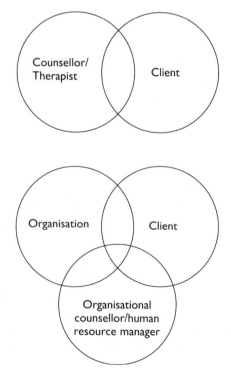

A discussion on the accepted ethical standards for general counselling practice does not fall within the scope of this book, and for further reading on this subject we would refer you to Appendix 2, which is a copy of the BAC's Code of Ethics and Practice. This is the standard reference for general professional practice in the United Kingdom. The purpose of this chapter is to highlight issues which bear specifically upon the ethics of counselling in organisations. We will now discuss these points in detail.

Six fundamental conditions are necessary to ensure sound ethical practice in the organisational context. They are these:

- a finely balanced ethical and political sensitivity
- clear operational guidelines
- understanding the nature of confidentiality
- high-quality training
- regular access to a professional supervisor
- an organisation counselling policy that is sympathetic, unambiguous, universally understood, and endorsed at the highest level.

Together these form the basis of a rounded approach to counselling in the organisation.

Ethical and political sensitivity

We are talking about two layers of sensitivity. The ethical refers to practice within the boundaries of a particular counselling relationship, which is a universal counselling concern, and is about the kind of question raised at the beginning of this chapter. The second is specific to workplace counselling. Whereas most counselling relationships are contracts between two people only – or a couple and one – in counselling within organisations there exists the presence of a third party to the contract – the party employing them both. This is the double-sided contract.

Potentially, this throws up the conflicts of interests and loyalties mentioned earlier. But we say potentially because we believe that it is, in fact, an issue that is readily solved by common sense. We may be even more provocative, and say that it has been overused by some members of the external provision lobby as a way of avoiding accountability and the intricacies of confidentiality 'within'.

Nevertheless, that potential for conflict does have implications that are profound and far-reaching. To illustrate the point, let us take the questions at the beginning of this chapter and set them into the context of the organisation:

'Might this person harm himself/someone else?' might become 'Is someone in the organisation harming this person? How far can it be addressed through empowering this person? At what point does it become an organisation issue?'

'Have I done as much as I can?' might become 'How far is the organisation bound to take the counselling process with this person?' Short-term focused work is often more effective than long-term work, but there are always exceptions. 'How much liberty do I take with the policy limits, in the best interests both of this person and of the organisation?'

The list goes on. And as in general counselling guidelines, there can be few hard-and-fast rules. Each situation is unique and requires judgement on its own merits. Perhaps one rule that can be applied is that no intervention is ever undertaken on the client's account without their full knowlege and consent.

This dimension is profound and far-reaching because, as well as containing the potential for conflict, it clearly carries with it enormous potential for conflict resolution. By influencing the context of a problem, counselling can become a form of mediation. It can bring the organisation and the individual together in ways inaccessible to anyone operating either within the organisation hierarchy, or fully external to the organisation.

For example, one employee went to the in-house counsellor complaining of bullying by her manager. After some 'reality-testing', ie asking how he was with others, and how others perceived him, the counsellor asked for – and was granted – her client's permission to discuss the matter with the human resources manager. The HR manager's response was one of relief: 'I have known for some time that something was terribly wrong in that department – now I know what it is'. The HR manager took the matter up with the bully's manager, and it was decided to raise his interpersonal style in an appraisal interview. The problem was then addressed at source, through counselling and counselling skills training for the bullying manager, with a satisfactory outcome for all concerned. This situation and others like it are quite common in the experience of internal counsellors.

It can make counselling vulnerable to manipulation though, both by clients and the organisation. Counsellors may occasionally come under pressure from people in the organisation who require information they believe might be useful to them. They are effectively kept at bay by a formal policy which establishes the counselling system as independent, or free-floating within the organisation, and by the professionalism of the counsellors themselves.

Any professional counsellor worth his or her salt will recognise these threats to confidentiality, and fend them off firmly enough to establish a solid base of credibility. He or she will also develop the nous to know when direct intervention is necessary (as in the story above), when and what issues need to be fed back into the organisation, and how to do so without any compromise in confidentiality.

This is something the external providers have consistently failed to do, and it is a vital element of a robust and fully effective counselling strategy. Some are beginning to get their acts together in this regard, but because of the way they are set up, by definition they are too far removed from the grass roots to provide the same quality of feedback. Their feedback remains mostly statistical.

There is one final caveat that belongs in this section, which is a matter of personal maturity and professional development. In talking about counselling, we are talking about the use of power. Counselling skills are powerful, and as such are open to abuse by people with agendas of their own, other than the well-being of the client. The only safeguards against this kind of manipulation are in supervision, and in the awareness and moral responsibility of the individual practitioner. Supervision in the counselling sense does not mean the same as supervision in the traditional sense. It refers to professional 'back up', a kind of second counsellor, once removed. Awareness and moral responsibility are defined as the qualities of respect, empathy and genuineness. They are the central characteristics required in the use of these skills, and we refer to them frequently during the course of the book. The selection of candidates for professional counselling training can be very tough, and rightly so. In fact, the degree of rigour in selection is a good indication of the quality of the training. This is not possible for large-scale training in counselling skills, and so the emphasis is different. Those who are unable to come to terms with the core values during the training, should be 'deselected', or discouraged from continuing.

It will also be seen from the above that the counsellor will need a sharp sense of professional priorities, as well as negotiating and influencing skills.

All of the issues we have discussed thus far are important, though not amenable to policy regulation. The issues that follow are those that should become policy-regulated procedure.

Operational guidelines

Wherever counselling is practised, whether it be in clinical settings, private practice or the workplace, there is a basic framework that remains more or less constant throughout. This framework concerns the limits of any one counsellor, and the way in which the boundaries (both practical and relational) are structured.

Limits (and beyond)

The range of issues presented to the workplace counsellor will, by definition, be very broad. Certain jobs and certain kinds of organisations will predispose to particular kinds of problems. But by and large the workplace represents the whole pageant of humanity in all its glorious diversity, and complete with its normal condition of *angst*. So the workplace counsellor will tend to be a generalist rather than a specialist.

For the counsellor, one of the most important things to remember about this, is: you do not have to make everyone better.

Note it well. Indeed, you do not *make* anyone better. The

desire to be someone's saviour, to take away all their unhappiness is a little vanity, a misconceived burden that besets every counsellor from time to time – especially in the early days of practice when one is least equipped so to do. Not even an experienced counsellor in a specialist agency is able to resolve everyone's problems – and that is not the brief. Remember that the purpose of counselling is to provide a safe place and the relevant skills to help someone explore and resolve their own difficulties and live in a more satisfying way. A very important part of that skill is to know your own limits and how to refer on when you feel you have reached them. When in doubt, seek supervision.

Be clear, too, about the limits of your brief. Consult organisational policy on the limit of their expectation and never be tempted to exceed it.

For the policy-maker, the organisation needs to be clear about what it expects from each level of counselling resource it is contracting to provide. For instance, it would be unrealistic at best, and dangerous at worst, to expect a human resources or personnel manager, who has had some brief training in counselling skills, to deliver more than first-stage work and an appropriate referral if more work is necessary.

It is also unrealistic to expect a single counsellor to be a panacea across the full range of problems that might come up. Provision needs to be made for a referral network that includes specialists, especially in the fields of legal, financial and medical advice. The practical considerations around establishing this network are a strategic concern, covered in the previous chapter.

Boundaries

Practical boundaries are all about containment. A large part of the therapeutic effect of counselling is tied up with safety, and not just the reality but also the perception of safety in the eyes of the client. The fear of exposing some kind of 'weakness' is such that, even with outside agencies, people have been known to drive quite long distances to seek help in another town where there is less chance of being recognised. One enlightened company director (who has gone public on his whole-hearted support of counselling in his multinational organisation) made a regular 60-mile round trip away from the workplace when his own marriage was going through a rocky patch. This demonstrates well that when the people outside the counselling room door are those on whom you depend for your livelihood, and also for large chunks of your status and self-esteem, not to mention your performance appraisal, that perceived threat can be acute enough to prevent someone taking the help that is on offer.

There are a number of ways in which this potential difficulty can be overcome. The first and most important is confidentiality, which we will deal with separately in the following section. The second is the issue of boundaries – both physical and relational.

The frame – as the space-and-time boundary is known in the jargon – is of critical importance for all the reasons we have just mentioned. If the counselling consists of one or two informal sessions with an HR professional (with whom one might just as well have other business), then the only real requirement is a sound-proof office, as no one else could know the purpose of the visits. At the other end of the scale, if a professional counsellor is employed to work regularly on-site then a room needs to be found that is discreetly positioned and without glass panels or paper-thin walls. This is also where a solidly reliable and trustworthy secretary is worth her weight in gold, acting as a liaison person and operating an appointments system, perhaps as part of a larger job.

Other options include an off-site venue. This loses some of the benefit of an in-house person, whose strength is partly in being a recognisable and accessible ally who is also well connected within the organisation (though this is implied in other ways if the counsellor is also an HR person employed full-time by the organisation).

The Wellness Forum idea provides another interesting possibility. If one might just as well be going for a massage or a weight-training workout as a counselling session, one has the benefit of anonymity as well as a positive association of ideas. Some organisations circumvent the question altogether by employing an off-the-peg, external resource or full-scale EAP. This does have some advantages but, as already discussed, we believe that on balance the loss is greater than the gain in terms of effectiveness.

All of the above presupposes, of course, that those using the counselling service are going to be shy about it. This is less true now than ever before. Many brave souls have been pushing back the barriers of prejudice by demonstrating openly that confronting one's worries and talking about them, rather than concealing them and hoping they will go away on their own, is really the only sensible thing to do.

Nevertheless, discretion will – and must – always be the order of the day.

The time frame is a less conspicuous yet still very important consideration. Providing unlimited time might seem like a generous thing to do. Therapeutically and organisationally though, it is both impossible and inefficient.

From a client's point of view there is a subtle sense of safety and containment brought about by the gentle discipline of time boundaries. Clinical practitioners operate what is known in the trade as a '50-minute hour'. This gives them time to disengage from one client and prepare for the next. It is quite rigorously applied – sometimes even mid-sentence – but very soon becomes customary and expected.

Different theoretical approaches believe quite different things regarding the overall amount of time anyone should spend in counselling, and individual counsellors within that differ, too. In general we would suggest that short-term focused work is an appropriate remit for an organisation. Anything beyond ten sessions, except in special circumstances, perhaps becomes the responsibility of the employee to seek out privately. This is a judgement that must remain with the counsellor in consultation with both her client and her supervisor.

Relationship boundaries Most professions have strict codes of conduct regarding relationships between practitioners and their clients, and counselling is no exception. This can sometimes be quite problematical in the counselling relationship, because the intensity of the contact, the personal nature of the information under discussion and the vulnerability of the client when they come for help all combine to draw the client and counsellor into a powerful interaction. In addition, counsellors can themselves be vulnerable at times and are especially so in the early and inexperienced years of the work.

Workplace relationships are often a web of old animosities and attractions, rivalry, ambition and political intrigue, alongside which the counselling ethos of empathy, congruence and impartiality sits quite uncomfortably. The anxiety about revealing 'weaknesses', or stepping out of the mould of the organisation's expectations of us, makes approaching a line manager or even a personnel manager about a personal problem an extraordinarily difficult thing to do. The anxiety may indeed be quite justified. Separating out the knowledge of a person's professional performance from knowledge of their personal circumstances may be quite difficult for a manager to do.

From the manager's point of view the boundary distinctions between the 'real' job and the counselling role may be equally tricky to negotiate. Lending a kindly ear for one or two sessions is one thing; taking on the burden of expectation for a full counselling commitment is quite another, particularly if in the process one's own role identity becomes confused.

From this it becomes apparent that whilst it may be desirable for in-company employees who are part of the hierarchical structure to practise some counselling skills, the appropriate role is in filtering cases either for referral onward, or for dealing with cases themselves on a practical or first-stage skill level.

Confidentiality and accountability

This subject really belongs with the discussion about boundaries and containment, but it is important enough to warrant a section on its own. Most people have the sense to understand that watertight confidentiality is a precondition of counselling but, as they say, 'there is always one'.

There is a true story of a personnel manager who spent some time counselling an employee. She began to be pressured to break confidentiality by the employee's line manager who, it later transpired, was anxious because he thought he was being talked about. The personnel manager refused to

Figure 4
A MODEL FOR COUNSELLING PROVISION

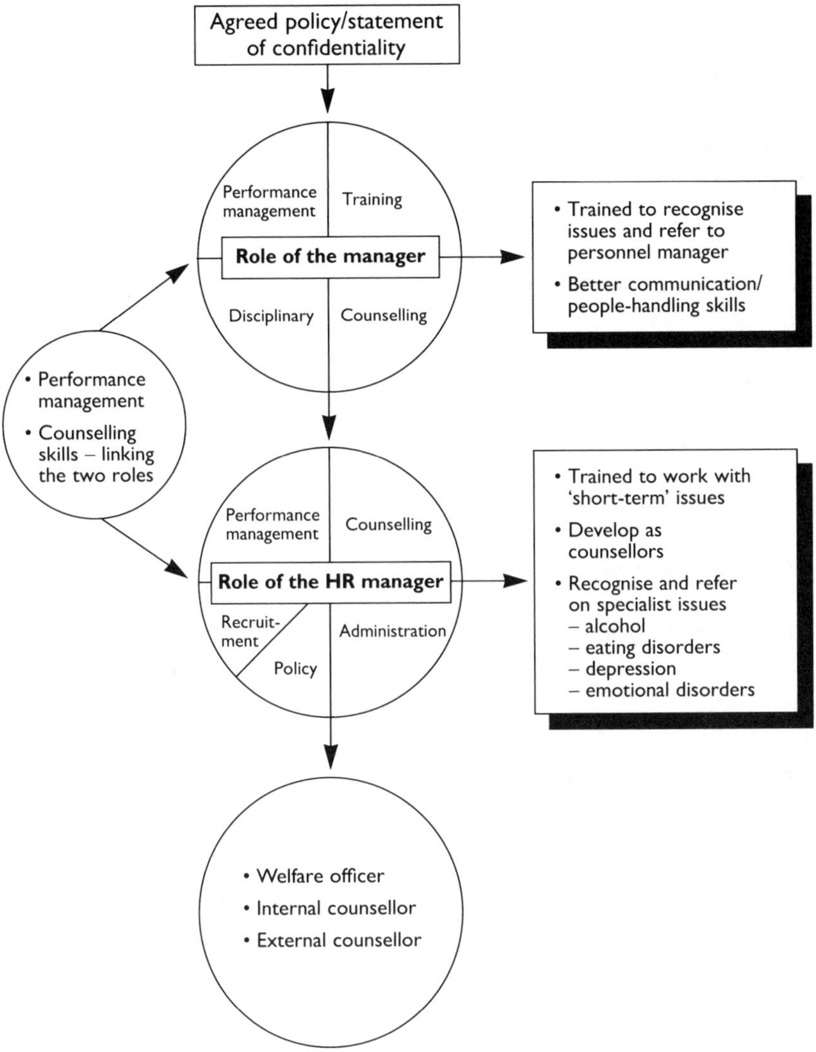

Agreed policy/statement
of confidentiality

Performance management | Training

Role of the manager

Disciplinary | Counselling

• Trained to recognise issues and refer to personnel manager

• Better communication/ people-handling skills

• Performance management
• Counselling skills – linking the two roles

Performance management | Counselling

Role of the HR manager

Recruit-ment | Administration

Policy

• Trained to work with 'short-term' issues

• Develop as counsellors

• Recognise and refer on specialist issues
  – alcohol
  – eating disorders
  – depression
  – emotional disorders

• Welfare officer
• Internal counsellor
• External counsellor

acknowledge even that the employee had come in for counselling. Having been successfully stonewalled, the irate manager went to complain to the chief executive, who in turn had the sense to back the personnel manager. That would have been the end of the story, had not that same line manager come in for counselling not long after. It was there that his own insecurities emerged. He had tested the system and found it safe enough to use himself.

The legal situation *vis-à-vis* confidentiality is clearly explained in the BAC Code of Ethics. (See Appendix 2.) The code does also say, though, that 'counsellors who have line managers owe them appropriate managerial accountability for their work'. The key word here is *appropriate*. Our belief is that whether or not there is a line manager, the counselling function does owe its employer some accountability.

It is vital that an organisation be able to control the quality of service it provides to its employees, as well as keeping a finger on the pulse of the causes of poor functioning in the organisation – especially if the aim is to address the causes of unhappiness as well as its effects. There is, however, a very clear line between the nature of information required for manipulative purposes, and for the purposes of monitoring quality.

It is also worth noting at this point that the counselling contract, though inviolate, is not the priest's confessional. Where someone is clearly in danger themselves it may well be appropriate to intervene more directly in their circumstances. This is a case-by-case judgement. Where they present a clear danger to others, however, there is a 'duty to warn'. This would be equally true for external or internal providers. We return to this later in the chapter.

External providers who present confidentiality as a reason for not contracting-in are being disingenuous. As long as counselling skills practitioners in the organisation are protected by policy, confidentiality can be kept *and* be seen to be kept. Experience has taught us that initial fears about disclosure are quickly dispelled once an in-house system is up and running. Organisations are, in fact, highly sensitive to, and respectful of, the confidentiality issue.

An in-house system is accountable, moreover. The ground rules and pathways for that accountability are for each individual organisation to set up with its own counselling function, and that counselling function must remain accountable to its clients for the way it sets up its boundaries. A solid foundation for good practice is laid down only when this framework of checks and balances is securely built into the system; when the counselling function is universally seen as independent and free-floating; and when good working relationships have been built up between counsellors and organisations. Given these conditions, and the required degree of professionalism, confidentiality is not a problem!

Training

Full counselling training, and counselling skills training, are covered in greater detail in the third part of this book. While we are considering ethics, though, it is important to mention three brief points in this regard.

1   Is there an ethical content built into the design of the programme you are using? There needs to be. It should cover general guidelines; give very clear boundaries about what level of counselling skills it sets out to provide (what its participants could and, more important, should not take on when they leave the course); and clarify the organisation's counselling policy on limits and expectations.

2   Is there provision for ongoing training? A single three- or five-day course does not make a counsellor, nor even a counselling skills practitioner. The training process is an ongoing one. In order to retain and develop the skills acquired, 'refreshers' are desirable; in order to maintain safe practice, they are essential.

3   Are the training courses run by qualified counsellors, or by professional trainers? However good trainers may be at training, they also will need to have experience of counselling to cope with the specialist content, and especially with the emotional content that inevitably emerges. Counselling training and even counselling skills training is not the same as other training.

There is one other, more general point, and it is this: counselling skills training needs to be linked into the professional counselling provision in order to provide a co-ordinated function. One HR manager who called in an external consultant to run counselling skills training, ensured that occupational health and in-house professional counsellors attended the course, which was primarily for HR people. In this way everyone involved with counselling was able to see how their role fitted in with everyone else's. There are, of course, other ways of achieving this cohesion.

The drawing up of criteria for the selection of professional in-house counsellors, and trainers from outside, is also an important consideration in assuring an acceptable level of quality. Certain kinds of training and orientation are more appropriate to the organisation context than others, and this is covered in greater detail in Chapter 4. Counsellors working within organisations will also need an intuitive ability and the right mind-set to function between the very different worlds of commerce and counselling, bridging the two. This will require a personal and professional flexibility, with the imagination and courage to find new ways of applying their skills and finding solutions to problem areas that are not well-worn in traditional counselling practice.

Professional supervision

Regular access to professional supervision is the *sine qua non* of all sound counselling practice, whether in or out of organisations. For the client it is the vital safeguard; for the counsellor it is an important mechanism of ongoing training, as well as the only opportunity for professional support and one-step-removed second opinion; for the organisation it is the most effective means of quality assurance available, quality audits included.

If you are employing a professional counsellor, ask if they work with a supervisor. (If the answer is no they are in breach of the code.) In selecting a professional supervisor, ask questions about training, experience, accreditation by professional bodies (as opposed to membership of, which means nothing) and, very importantly, their degree of understanding and experience of commercial organisations. Don't compromise.

And in setting up counselling policy, be sure to make adequate provision for supervision support. Supervisors will usually be most effective if they are independent of the organisation, as opposed to the counsellors, who will usually be most effective working from within the organisation. In our view, this is in many ways the ideal combination.

It would be difficult to overstate the importance of high quality supervision, not least because of the inexorable movement towards litigation by employees. Adequate supervision is, and will remain, the most universally regarded evidence of responsible practice.

Policy

We have offered a thorough-going list of considerations that need to be taken into account when setting up an in-house counselling policy. (We reserve comment about external providers, because all of the areas discussed leave the control of the organisation once the subscription is paid.) All that remains is to ensure that once the organisation has identified its needs and thought through the issues, the result is embedded in a formal counselling policy.

At the beginning of the chapter, we described the policy as 'sympathetic, unambiguous, universally understood, and endorsed at the highest level'. This is self-explanatory with the exception of 'universally understood'. By this we mean that, as all employees across all levels are potential users of the system, all should have access to the reassurance that such a solid document would offer. Exactly how that is done – whether in marketing the system or more discreetly – remains a choice for each organisation.

Self-regulation, along the guidelines set out above, is a convincing demonstration of an organisation's commitment to provide the best possible care for its employees. This squeaky-cleanness is a matter of growing importance.

Counselling and the law

Not strictly an issue of ethics, but one that is closely related, is law. The law is a relatively new presence in the field of workplace counselling, and is therefore still largely an untested and unknown quantity. However, it is becoming evident that there are strong implications for organisations, whether they employ counselling or not. On the one hand, there are knotty problems around possessing information that is dangerous, and not dealing with it properly in the eyes of the law. On the other hand, pleading ignorance of either the problem or the law is no defence.

There are some areas that require careful consideration and, if you are worried, legal advice:

Duty to warn

To the authors' knowledge, there has been no case involving this in the UK to date. Mental health specialists in the USA are required to disclose confidential information if it presents 'clear and present danger'. As the legal consequences seem unclear in the UK, it is hard to comment on what might happen if a counsellor did not warn someone whom they believed their client would harm. Examples of this would be if a client said they were going to murder someone, or to continue having unprotected sexual intercourse after being diagnosed as HIV positive.

Prevention of Terrorism Act

Here at least the law is quite clear. Counsellors, either formal or HR/line managers temporarily in the counselling role, who suspect that an act of terrorism has or will take place are committing a treasonable offence by not informing the police. Professional counsellors should know that the contract of confidentiality with their clients is not the same as a priest's confessional.

The law and stress claims

There is panic in some quarters about litigation, arising out of a recent court finding. One article talks about a 'wave of stress claims' being forecast by city lawyers.

What many fail to mention about the now famous case of Walker v. Northumberland County Council, is that it is unique in many respects. The most important point is that Walker had had a previous nervous breakdown prior to the one that led to the court action. Medical evidence existed that provided clear proof that psychiatric injury was *caused* by his job. Other claims may be highly speculative if they lack such clear proof, but claims may be made in the hope that employers will pay just to be rid of the bad publicity. Both employees and employers should be aware that a steep rise in successful claims may seriously affect the ease with which employers' liability insurance can be obtained. Both parties need to beware of irresponsible generalisations and victory cries, conditional fees being offered by lawyers, and general confrontation and demand-type approaches.

We do not presume to give legal advice, but there are three precautions we would recommend:

☐ Do not automatically assume counsellors are familiar with the law.

☐ Include legal aspects in counselling skills training, and provide information to professional counsellors who do not have training in this respect.

☐ Seek specialist legal advice if you are in any doubt, and especially if you recognise any of the above situations.

Clearly the sane response to all of this is to view the reduction of unnecessary stress in organisations as being intrinsically valuable, and to take a thoughtful and methodical approach to the issues we have raised. The value is not just to increase productivity and reduce absenteeism, but to enhance employee well-being.

We have acknowledged that setting up has many aspects and requires careful planning. Provided that purposes and procedures are carefully considered in advance, embedded in training and policy, and checked and balanced by professional supervision, these challenges can be met. Once the system is successfully in place, maintaining it becomes relatively straightforward.

Counselling is, above all, the art of the possible.

PART 2

FACE TO FACE

4

COUNSELLING SKILLS FOR

THE WORKPLACE

Counselling at work is about three things:

- counselling *per se*, usually short-term, to resolve specific problems
- creating better interpersonal relationships
- other types of 'advice', on legal, financial or medical problems.

The first of these categories requires face-to-face work either by a professional counsellor, or by a skills-trained HR professional, depending on the nature and complexity of the problem.

The second category refers to the use of good communication skills in the management of day-to-day workplace relationships. At the most fundamental level, counselling skills are about effective communication, and in this context they are also relevant to a wide range of organisation processes such as mentoring, coaching, change management, mediation, etc.

The third category is not counselling, technically speaking, because counsellors do not give advice. Legal, financial and medical advisers have their primary training in those disciplines, though they will need to have training in counselling skills too in order to help clients cope with the emotional difficulties that can arise when life goes wrong in one of these areas. Financial difficulties in particular are among the commonest causes of suicide and suicide attempts, often among people who can seem to be coping quite well with life and holding down responsible jobs. Money advice and debt restructuring are practical, participative and, therefore, very labour-intensive forms of helping. Because of their high degree of specialism we will not cover these areas in the book, but recommend agencies that serve the wider community, such as Citizens Advice Bureaux, for their excellent work in both legal and money advice.

Though all three purposes will be represented in some way in a fully comprehensive network of employee support, it is the first two that are the focus of our interest in this book.

Counselling skills training gives people a framework and a set of skills that will enable them to give help to others. The skills themselves are communication tools that can be assimilated into a management style and called up in an infinite number of situations. When they are placed within a counselling framework, the skills become a more structured helping process, and this is what is meant by 'first-stage skills' or 'first-level counselling'.

Full counselling demands a full-time professional training, experience, personal development, formal supervision and theoretical understanding. The use of counselling skills crosses over into full counselling at the point where theoretical models are applied to the interpretation of events in the client's life.

In each degree of skill use, practitioners have a duty to be aware of, and to observe the limits of, the help they are able to provide. Later in the chapter we will set out some basic guidelines to define the parameters of that help. First we will outline the Egan framework, and describe the basic skills. Then we will present five theoretical models that we believe to be the most useful for counselling in the workplace, and one that we do not. Our purpose here is to familiarise the reader with some of the terms and concepts, and discuss their appropriateness to the organisational setting.

No discussion of counselling in practice should begin without at least a mention of the core values. We mention these before we begin, because without them one should not enter into a helping relationship. Carl Rogers, who is widely regarded as the father of counselling, identified three main qualities of being, as conditions essential to the helping process. He called them empathy, congruence, and unconditional positive regard. *Empathy* means the ability to put oneself in another's shoes (as opposed to sympathy, which means to feel sorry for). Gerard Egan describes it as 'the ability to enter into and understand the world of another person and to communicate this understanding to him or her'.[1] *Congruence* is the quality of genuineness. We all recognise and respond to this intuitively when we find it in another person, yet it is hard to define. Perhaps the person who exudes congruence is the person who is at ease with him- or herself, and by definition this is not possible to fake. The only way to be congruent is to know and fully accept oneself, and to care genuinely for others. *Unconditional positive regard* is the suspension of all judgement on the other person, respecting them as individuals and their right to self-determination. To judge people, however 'good' one's motives, is to put them on the defensive. That erects a barrier and it aborts the whole helping process. When selecting people for counselling training it would be as well to keep these three qualities in mind. Later in the book we will refer to them as empathy, genuineness and respect (for convenience), and define the specific behaviours that go with these words.

It is in the nature of a manager's job to solve problems, and therefore one of the most difficult things for a natural manager to learn in helping skills is how to hold back from this impulse. There are times when action is called for on someone else's behalf, but counselling is seldom one of those. The goal of counselling is not to make everything all right, but to enable the other to manage their own problem situation. Egan points out that clients do not present *problems* in the mathematical sense of the word, 'because emotions usually run high and there are usually no clear-cut solutions. Clients face *problem situations* . . . troubles, doubts, difficulties, frustrations, or concerns . . . complex and often messy difficulties in living that they are not handling effectively.'[2] Solving another's problem situations – even if it were in our power to do so – might seem a useful thing to do in the short term, but in the longer term it creates or reinforces a learned helplessness. Counselling is the ultimate form of what has now become jargonised as 'empowerment'.

The framework

The framework gives a broad structure to the counselling process. It serves as a map to orientate the counsellor in the process and to give direction and purpose to any intervention he or she might make. This helps to ensure that interventions are considered, rather than random. The framework we offer here is the Egan Model, which is probably the most widely used across all settings, including the workplace. It is particularly useful in the workplace environment because its pragmatism and focus on problem-solving makes it useful for short-term counselling. Egan has outlined a three-stage model of helping that is rational, linear and systematic. This framework provides a structure and discipline to the process that is particularly helpful to those who are new to counselling. It is a structure in which all skills and theories can be used. As one grows in skill and practice it becomes evident that these are not rigid steps, but that they overlap and interweave. Even for experienced counsellors, though, they act as a useful anchor and reference point.

Stage one: exploring and clarifying

The first task in being able to manage one's own problem situation is to identify it clearly and understand it more fully.

The *steps* in this stage are:

- *Helping clients tell their stories*
  - contract on confidentiality, purpose and time constraints
  - building rapport
  - exploring the present scenario

- *Focusing*
  - identifying and clarifying problem situations/unused opportunities
  - screening – looking for areas of leverage

- *Looking for new perspectives*
  - finding other frames of reference
  - challenging (or 'confronting') the blind spots

and the *skills* are:

- Showing acceptance/empathy *
- Allowing emotions *
- Giving full attention
- Active listening *
- Reflecting back *
- Summarising *
- Reframing (paraphrasing) *
- Appropriate questioning *
- Understanding the salient issues
- Asking for clarification
- Observing posture and body language
- Focusing *
- Following threads, developing details
- Noticing and challenging discrepancies ('confronting') *

The above are what is meant when 'first-level counselling' or 'first-stage skills' are referred to. These can be very powerful in themselves, because seeing a problem situation more clearly is sometimes all a client needs to release him or her to act. Surprisingly often, people will express gratitude simply at being listened to, sometimes for what seems to them to be the first time.

These skills can also be regarded as good lifeskills which can be constructively used in many situations other than counselling, such as the management situations we have mentioned.

* The asterisk after some of the skills indicates those on which we provide explanatory notes after this section. Some of the terms are self-explanatory. We have selected those whose meaning or use in this specific context may be unfamiliar.

Stage two: developing a preferred scenario and setting goals

Though some clients will be able to move forward simply by understanding what is holding them back, most will need to move on to the next stage which is to create, in a sense, a new world of possibilities to move into. Many people are locked into self-defeating patterns of thinking about themselves and the world, and cannot move on because they do not know where to go.

The *steps* in this stage are:

- *Constructing a new scenario*
  - clarifying the real issue
  - identifying key areas for change
  - setting new goals

- *Examining the options critically*
  - getting specific on goals
  - reviewing consequences
  - setting priorities

- *Making choices*

and the *skills* are:

- All the skills of stage one

  plus

- Identifying the key points
- Summarising and reflecting on key points
- Testing mutual understanding
- Balancing challenge and support
- Supporting ideas
- Immediacy * – using observations and sharing own reactions
- Specific strategies, eg Lewin's Force Field Analysis *

In practice, these steps do not fit quite so neatly into compartments. As progress is made through Stage Two, counsellor and client will often be revisiting stage one in the light of new information. This is the interweaving we talked about earlier. The process, though focused, will remain fluid if it is going well. When the end of Stage Two is reached, the client should have a clearer idea both of the difficulty and what he or she would like to accomplish, without necessarily knowing how to set about achieving it.

In some versions of this model Stage Two is represented as *clarifying*. People have tended to interpret the model according to their own needs: that is fine. It is not chiselled in stone, and in any case the process remains more or less the same, except that the lines are drawn in different places, and the names are different. Remember it is only a model. It is there to serve, not to dictate to the practitioner.

Stage three: action and problem-solving

Having goals does not automatically ensure that change is going to happen. The client and counsellor must now set about the task of translating new goals into plans, and then into reality. Again, the stage is approached in three phases:

The *steps* in this stage are:

- *Brainstorming strategies for action*
  - generate as many ideas as possible. Reject none, however crazy they may sound

- *Choosing strategies and formulating a plan*
  - review the list, reflect on the options
  - find one, or a combination, that appeals to the client and suits his or her resources

- *Action*
  - review 'facilitating and restraining' forces
  - facilitate support and encourage the implementation of plans

and the *skills* are:

- Motivating and encouraging
- Using specific strategies, eg Lewin's Force Field Analysis

The skills

Empathy

Strictly speaking, empathy is more a core quality (as outlined previously), than a skill. Empathy is listening carefully, understanding the core messages, and communicating that understanding accurately to the client. This involves a combination of all of the first-stage skills and it is a vital component of effective communication. Though the skills can be learned, there is an 'X' factor that turns empathy from a collection of skills into a way of being. That factor is a certain maturity that has less to do with age than with an absence of egocentricity.

Allowing emotions

Many people find it terribly daunting to be faced with someone who is weeping copiously or displaying anger, or some other kind of high emotion. Much discomfort is simply about not knowing how to react. How does one 'allow' emotion?

Crying

Don't say
– 'We'll sort this out when you've calmed down' and then back off.
– 'It's OK to cry.' This only raises the possibility that it may not be. (Exception is when someone is apologising for crying.)
– 'I understand.' In all probability you don't, yet, and it is likely to make your client feel more misunderstood than anything else (see reflecting back, etc.).
–'Don't cry.' This reveals more concern for your own discomfort than for your client's.

Do say
– nothing, wait patiently for the crying to subside (which it will, eventually!) and then say, gently, something like: 'Can you tell me what is making you so sad?' or 'I see that something (or this) is very painful for you,' or 'I see you are very unhappy,' or 'I am sorry this is so difficult for you', etc.; ie an observation of the situation, or a gentle invitation to speak. This may of course set the person off again, but that is fine –

you have not upset them further. You have given them permission to feel the way they do. Just wait patiently again and when it subsides, say 'Do you feel better able to talk about it now?' Remember crying is just a way of letting off steam. It is a healthy – and healing – response.

Anger When a client is venting a lot of anger in the counselling room, try to remember that she or he is unlikely to be angry with you, although it may be directed at you. You are bound to feel defensive, but keep calm. Use the observational question: 'This is making you very angry, isn't it?' or 'Can we look at what it is about this situation that is making you so angry?' This is using the skill of reflecting – see later section. In extreme circumstances, for example if you are feeling physically threatened, don't put yourself at risk. Suggest you meet when the person has calmed down, then leave. Do not meet again until you have spoken to your professional (counselling) supervisor.

Active listening

Everyone has experienced the extreme irritation of speaking to someone who is pretending to listen, whilst clearly being so busy formulating their own speech they cannot wait for the speaker to end. Equally annoying are those who do not even bother to pretend. At a subliminal level we are all very much aware of the signals of non-attention and the barriers they set up to effective communication, though few of us recognise our own shortcomings in this regard. The OED defines *hearing* as 'perceiving sounds with the ear'. *Listening,* on the other hand, is to 'hear with attention . . . give ear to' . This expresses beautifully the fact that listening is as much about giving something (attention) as it is about receiving something (the speaker's meaning). Real listening is never passive, even though one may be sitting quite still. Active listening, or attending, means taking in all the information that is available – both verbally and non-verbally. It involves noticing things like posture, facial expression, movement and tone of voice as well as what is being said and what is being half-said, or hinted at, or conspicuously omitted. Often you will notice discrepancies between what is being said and the behaviour that is being displayed. These observations can be used in conjunction with the skill of immediacy (see page 76). Active listening also means showing actively that you are listening by your own non-verbal behaviour. This signalling of acceptance (eye contact, nodding, uh-huhing, facial responses, etc.) happens quite spontaneously when we are genuinely absorbed in what someone is saying. In situations by which we might not normally be swept along, it is the by-product of the discipline of active listening. Initially this discipline is surprisingly hard work. This author remembers well the exhaustion of the first few professional counselling sessions, after which it was necessary to go home and take a nap! The good news is that, like any muscle regularly used, attention of this quality soon comes so easily that it becomes second nature. You will know you've cracked it when you are able to make detailed notes of a complex conversation a week after it has taken place.

One final word about active listening: this degree of intensity in listening is not appropriate to all situations and all interactions. Along with the ability to use this skill, comes the natural ability to switch it on and off, as and when necessary.

Reflecting back

This, and the skills of summarising and reframing, are all ways of checking that you have understood accurately, and also of showing acceptance and empathy by demonstrating that you are 'being with' your client.

Reflecting back – as the name suggests – is repeating, in more or less the same words, what your client has said to you. The effect of this skill on the client is similar to that of hearing our voices played back on a tape recorder. It sounds different when we say things ourselves, because we are hearing the sound from inside our heads, as well as through the outer ear. When that same sound is played back to us through another instrument, it is no longer distorted by the inner echo and we hear it in a different way. Perceptually speaking, the counsellor acts as that external voice when he 'plays back', or *reflects back* what we have said. Sometimes what we have said seems to take on quite a different significance when someone else says it. This does *not* mean parroting everything that is being said, which could have consequences quite opposite to those we desire. Often it is just one word reflected as a question. This is a 'prompt' that invites someone to explore the meaning of what they have just said without asking a question that might be intrusive. Or you can reflect both what the client says, 'So everyone in your group is ignoring you,' *and* how the client seems to feel about it, 'and it sounds as though you are feeling very isolated.' It is a good idea to try to pick up how the client is feeling, and help him put it into words. It encourages the client to confirm, or elaborate, or adjust his meaning. It is also another way of signalling your acceptance – empathy, or being in the other's world.

Reflecting back as a way of signalling acceptance, can be non-verbal too. If you observe two people getting along really well you will often notice that they mirror each other's body language quite unconsciously. Done consciously, this can become quite ridiculous, and we are not suggesting this is what you should do. But occasionally the natural process goes wrong, and this needs to be consciously changed. For instance, a manager who was on communications training for 'breaking the news' in preparation for downsizing, had been puzzled that he seemed to be upsetting people whenever he most wanted to be sensitive. He had to be told that he had an unfortunate way of grimacing when he was being sympathetic that made him look (ironically) as though he was smiling. Consciously altering this response made all the difference.

Summarising and reframing
Summarising is used after a number of points have been made . . . 'May I just check that I have understood this correctly . . .?' It draws together the key points and ideas that have been mentioned. The counsellor takes time and care to find the core of what the client is saying, and offers it back in an abbreviated form. This both confirms and anchors the story thus far, reassures the client that he is being heard accurately, and thus allows him to move on to the next stage. Like reflecting, it also gives the client a chance to correct any misconstruing on the part of the counsellor. This can be used in different ways, and at different points in the process. It is one of the skills of focusing (see page 73):

☐ In Stage One (exploring and clarifying), after several points have been made. Here it 'punctuates' the client's story, giving it form and consolidating it. It helps the counsellor too, in testing meaning and committing the story to memory. The summaries are always tentative, starting with phrases like 'Are you saying that . . .?' or 'It sounds like . . .'

☐ In Stages One and Two, (clarifying; developing a preferred scenario and setting goals), to help the client see links and contrasts between the different things they are saying. This is a powerful way of clarifying issues. It helps distinguish their relative importance, or the 'figure and ground' of a situation. As in a good painting, the important 'figures' will come forward, and the background will recede. Because we are describing a process, it is a moving picture; different features come forward and recede continually. This is true also of summarising in the following context.

☐ At the end of a stage. Here the counsellor summarises to reflect on the work done so far, in order to move on into the next stage. Remember that in practice these stages are not 'cut and dried', as they are presented here.

Reframing is 'counsellorspeak' for paraphrasing, or saying the same thing in an altogether different way. The difference between this and summarising is subtle. These statements will sometimes start with phrases like, 'It sounds almost as though . . .' (very similar to tentative summarising, but from a different angle). Metaphors can be used here to good effect. The vivid mind-picture created by an accurate metaphor can be a powerful expression of a client's situation, giving a new and often quite liberating perspective. For instance, one warring couple was told they reminded their counsellor of a pair of curled-up hedgehogs. This enabled each to relate to the other's vulnerability, instead of reacting only to their defences. It also moved the work out of an impasse, and along several paces.

If you get it right, the skill of reframing can give the client quite another slant on his thinking and the response is often one of excitement, or even gratitude for feeling understood. It is affirming, encouraging and can open a whole new aspect of understanding.

Appropriate questioning

Appropriate use of questioning is the most valuable tool a helper has in the task of gathering information and clarifying.

Appropriate is the operative word. We have all been on the receiving end of inappropriate questions – nosey, intrusive questions; aggressive, accusing questions; and the infuriating 'why?' questions reminiscent of a bored five-year-old. 'Why' questions can be used, but only very prudently. Or frame them in an indirect way: say, 'Why do you suppose that . . .' or, 'Have you any clues as to why . . .'. A direct 'why' pins the client down. It implies that a person should know the answers, and the reason they are in counselling is very often precisely because they don't! This is less applicable in the straightforward use of skills in day-to-day management situations, where 'why' may be a perfectly acceptable form of question. It should still be used with care, however.

Clearly, some variations of form and content are not appropriate in counselling. Form is as important as content. It is important to consider the forms that questions can take.

Question types

Question/statement	Useful in counselling	Not useful in counselling
Open 'Tell me about . . .' 'How do you feel about . . .' Encourages the individual to talk.	Most openings. Exploring new areas and gathering information.	Where clarification is required.
Probe 'Exactly what skills were required for that job?' Vital for details; follows open question to obtain more detail.	For checking information.	Care is needed when exploring emotionally charged areas.
Closed 'Do you want to stay in this job . . .' Narrows context and establishes points of fact.	For probing single facts.	For gaining information in areas not yet fully explored.

Question/statement	Useful in counselling	Not useful in counselling
Reflective *'You seem to feel upset about this move.'* Very powerful. Repeats back the emotion and content of an individual's statement.	For establishing empathy and for exploring emotionally charged situations.	For checking information and facts.
Leading *'I suppose you feel more confident in an administrative position.'* Invariably leads to an expected response.	For gaining acceptance – if you believe this to be the case.	For gaining genuine information about the person.
Hypothetical *'What would you do if . . . ?'* Poses a hypothetical situation in the future.	For getting individuals to think about new areas or ideas.	With individuals who need time to give a reasoned response, ie they are still in Stage One and emotionally charged.
Multiple A string of questions/statements, without a break.	Never.	
Rhetorical A question which expects no answers.	In public meetings.	In one-to-one meetings.
Circular *'How did you use to feel about . . . ?'* 'Arcing' from past to present to future.	For Stage Two. Clarifying the situation.	In Stage One – when still exploring.
Triadic/Diadic *'How do you think your boss views the situation?'* Brings in view about others involved.	For Stage Two. Clarifying the picture.	In Stage One – when still exploring.

Focusing

The counselling process moves continually back and forth between exploratory, or 'opening out' phases, and focusing, or 'narrowing down' phases. When the work is in a stage of exploration, techniques (like some of those above) are used to

open out the field of enquiry; when the work moves into a stage where clarification of a point is necessary, narrowing down or focusing techniques are used. Egan uses the term *focusing* to describe looking for points of high leverage, by which he means finding that point of balance – or issue – that will create the greatest shift in a situation, with the least 'force'. But the term can also be used to mean developing specific areas of the picture, following a single line of detailed enquiry that might be fruitful by means of, for instance, probing-type questions. The three skills used most frequently for the purpose of focusing are:
– closed or probing questions
– summarising
– accurate empathy.

Clients who ramble endlessly can present a problem. Egan says: 'Rambling destroys the concreteness, the focus and the intensity of the helping experience. If the helper punctuates the client's ramblings with nods, "uh-huhs" and the like, the rambling is merely reinforced. Monologues on the part of either helper or client are ordinarily not helpful. Therefore, the counsellor should respond relatively frequently to the client, without interrupting what is important or making the client lose his or her train of thought. Frequent use of accurate empathy and timely use of probes give a great deal of direction to the counselling process.'[3]

Some helpers are concerned about giving offence by interrupting, but it can be done quite inoffensively: 'Do you mind if we return to something you said a few minutes ago that seemed quite important . . .?' or 'I would just like to check out my understanding of what you have been saying so that I do not lose anything important.' Then summarise and ask a specific or probing-type question that focuses the next part of the conversation. Experience will give the practitioner a feel for helping this kind of client to focus, and may be one of the most valuable things you can do for someone whose chaotic habits of thinking might well be a large part of their problem.

Challenging and confronting

These words are used interchangeably, and they mean the same thing in the end. We are referring to the skill of recognising and *gently* pointing out logical inconsistencies. This requires a lot of skill in order to avoid a defensive reaction. Done well, it is a powerful way of opening up new insights for the client.

When two statements are taken out of the narrative and juxtaposed, they will often bring into sharp focus some contradiction, or make some previously unrecognised connection. Challenging is not just about inconsistencies in the story, however. It is also about inconsistencies between what a person is saying, or how they perceive themselves or their situations, and what the observer hears or sees.

This is risky territory; it is also essential. It is essential because if people don't know what is not working for them, they cannot change it. One senior manager, who thought his style was jovial, was fired because he was really coming across as bullying. A human resources person is in the ideal situation to tackle this kind of problem, because she or he is removed from the line. Where someone has relationship problems, and no one ever has the courage to address it with them in a constructive way, they will always need to move on. Avoiding challenge is a cop-out. The counsellor or HR manager who avoids challenge is not doing the best for their client or colleague.

Because challenging can be so risky, there are some 'rules' about approaching it:
– Whether it is used in a full counselling or 'first-line' situation, it should not be done without thoroughly exploring and listening first. Where someone is not even aware they have a problem, it will take a high degree of diplomacy to get them into a helping situation in the first place. So the first rule is: not too early. The client (or colleague) needs to be able to hear what you are saying, and this requires some relationship of trust which is built by first-stage skills.
– Go gently. Challenge needs to be balanced with support.
– Remember, you can also confront someone with their strengths. There are many people who consistently undervalue themselves. Whatever their reasons for doing this – and this may well be worth exploring in a counselling interview – they will need to be given a more realistic view of themselves.

Immediacy

This is a skill that requires acute observation both of others and oneself, and a willingness to be open. The helper uses his or her own responses to give the client another perspective to explore:

☐ perhaps how their behaviour impacts on others: 'When you said that to me, I found myself feeling really quite threatened even though I know you didn't mean to have that effect. I wonder if sometimes your staff feel that way too . . .'

☐ how to get in touch with a feeling they may not have recognised: 'Whenever you talk about your brother I start to feel sad. Have you any idea why I should feel that way . . .?'

☐ when there is some discrepancy between what the client is saying and the other signals you are getting: 'Your words are telling me you are fine, but your voice is telling me that you're not.'

This last intervention could also be described as 'accurate empathy'. The first and last could also be called challenging, or confronting. The process as a whole is fluid rather than rigid, and developing a fluency with the skills helps you to call on them effortlessly when they are needed. In this way they become integrated into your repertoire of spontaneous responses, and they can be used in a variety of contexts.

When you use the skills, you are making an intervention. You cannot make an intervention without using the skills.

When the helping process is moving along nicely, the basic skills we have mentioned here will be woven easily into the conversation in such a way that they become almost unnoticeable. From time to time however, the process will become a bit stuck, will go round in circles, or get a little lost. Even in the best-managed encounters this will happen, and when it does the helper needs to stand back from the process to review where it is going, or how to move it along faster, or redirect it. At such times specific strategies might be used in analysing the work, or in changing its pace and focus. The following is one of many such strategies.

Lewin's Force Field Analysis

This is a simple technique that any helper can use with a client in the 'action' stage, to look at the forces that will either facilitate or restrain them in achieving the goals they have set for themselves. The technique may be divided up into seven steps, and it helps to work through them as a paper-and-pencil exercise:

1   As the first step it is necessary to have defined the specific change objective.
2   Help the client list all the restraining forces that might prevent them from achieving this objective.
3   On the right side of the page, do the same with all the facilitating forces at work which will help them to achieve the objective.
4   Grade or rate the restraining and facilitating forces on a scale of 1–5.
5   Identify which forces the client has control over, and disregard those they cannot influence at all.
6   Help the client to identify what they can do, firstly to decrease the larger restraining forces.
7   Then look at how to increase the smaller facilitating forces.

A practical consideration

Re-entering the day-to-day world after a counselling or intense 'helping' session can be difficult enough without freshly released emotions to contend with. For this reason a good counsellor will always use the last 15 minutes of a session to 'close down' difficult issues, rather than open them up. Even so, half-an-hour or so of quiet reflection somewhere after a session really helps a client to process some of the new thoughts and allow them to settle. This precaution is even more necessary in the workplace.

... and a point to ponder

The BAC Code of Ethics recognises the use of counselling skills as a discrete and highly pragmatic part of counselling practice by those temporarily in a helping role who are not the person's counsellor.

Some have argued that the use of counselling skills is meaningful only in a relational context, ie where they exist only as a part of a professional counselling training or formal counselling relationship. However, our experience of working with people in organisations is that when people start to use counselling skills, something remarkable happens. The very use of these skills creates a different relationship; that is, one based on empathy, genuineness and respect. They create better management practice and will support moves towards culture change, empowerment and the sharing of control by the creation of self-managing teams – all very real issues that organisations in the 1990s are grappling with (Summerfield, 1995).[4]

There is a specific context for ethical issues, roles and boundary demarcation in the use of skills where HR and line managers are concerned; different organisational roles require the use of different counselling skills, different 'contracts' and different 'depths' of training.

The real question, we believe, is not whether counselling skills should be used by non-professionals. It is this: At what point should the client be referred on?

The answer has three dimensions:

□   the nature of the problem
□   the nature of the relationship
□   the depth of training.

Nature of the problem
There is a whole category of problems that should never be tackled by anyone at a 'skills' level of help, except for the purpose of recognition and referral on to specialist help. These include most of those in the following chapter, such as drug and alcohol problems, eating disorder, marital difficulty, depression, etc. In such cases, the observant HR professional or line manager is often the first port in a storm. The exception is bereavement, which is one area in which a sensitive and informed skills-trained management professional is able to be of significant ongoing help. There are other areas (see Chapter 6) where it is desirable for a management professional to be on the alert and able to offer skills-level assistance. For ease of reference we offer the rough guide below. Do

remember though that it is a rough guide, and that the only real rule for managers in doubt is the golden one: when in doubt, don't. It is always better to refer on than to take on something you suspect might be beyond your depth of skill. See Figure 5.

Figure 5
GUIDE TO REFERRAL

Arrows indicate possible referral onwards; double arrows indicate areas where referral might move in either direction, or where two professionals might collaborate depending on the specific situation and confidentiality of the contract.

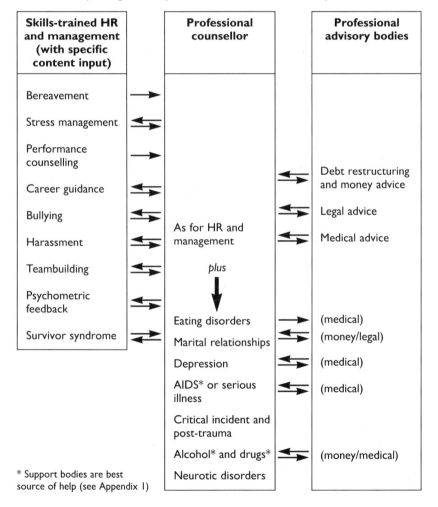

Skills-trained HR and management (with specific content input)	Professional counsellor	Professional advisory bodies
Bereavement →		
Stress management ⇄		
Performance counselling →		
Career guidance ⇄		⇄ Debt restructuring and money advice
Bullying ⇄		⇄ Legal advice
Harassment ⇄	As for HR and management	⇄ Medical advice
Teambuilding ⇄		
Psychometric feedback ⇄	*plus* ↓	
Survivor syndrome ⇄	Eating disorders	→ (medical)
	Marital relationships	⇄ (money/legal)
	Depression	⇄ (medical)
	AIDS* or serious illness	⇄ (medical)
	Critical incident and post-trauma	
	Alcohol* and drugs*	⇄ (money/medical)
* Support bodies are best source of help (see Appendix 1)	Neurotic disorders	

Nature of the relationship

This is a role boundary issue. When an organisational colleague is temporarily in the role of helper, there will always be a line between the client's private and professional interests. This will be particularly true where the lines of reporting and counselling responsibility overlap, though this can be eased to some extent by encouraging a lateral approach to the support structure. Nevertheless, there will always be a delicate balance to be struck between concern and intrusiveness, and the helper in an organisational role must remain sensitive to a client's boundaries of personal privacy. Where the relationship is exclusively that of professional counsellor to client, these concerns are far less likely to arise.

Therefore, at the skills-trained level of temporary helper, the referral onward point lies at:

☐ the client's boundary of private and professional interest
☐ the helper's boundary of counselling competency.

This relates to both the nature of problem, and also to the depth of training.

The depth of training

Where helping leaves the realms of the purely systematic and enters the realms of the theoretical and interpretative, it crosses the boundary from skills practice into professional counselling.

The framework of steps and skills we have outlined thus far are the focus of counselling skills training. Effectively taught, they will enable line and human resource managers to make a real difference in dealing with workplace issues, and also to refer on appropriately. Counselling skills training courses *must* make clear to all trainees the parameters of their training.

Professional counselling training goes much further in several important ways. Counsellors must have personal development, supervision and a depth of theoretical understanding in order to equip them to cope with more complex levels of difficulty. Some will work with only one theoretical perspective, or model; others will work with an eclectic mix. We have found some of these models to be more applicable to the workplace context, and the ones we have decided to include are Rogerian, Cognitive Behavioural, Personal Construct, Psychodynamic, Transactional Analysis, and Systems.

Theoretical models

These refer to the particular understanding, or 'model of man' that is being brought to bear on a given situation. They are presented for clarification only, as their use constitutes full-blown counselling – as opposed to the practice of counselling skills, or first-line counselling.

The first thing to know about the theories that underpin counselling, is that there are no absolute truths. The human condition is so wonderfully complex that we defy all attempts to impose scientific rigour and absolutes on our existence. Some theorists have tried to enlist scientific method to prove their ultimate rightness, but all have been thwarted. The reason is that most are right, but only partially. The truth is that every way of looking at the human mind is only a model. The solution is to be pragmatic; some models are more useful than others, but which is which depends on the context and the purpose for which it is to be used. Our context is the workplace, and our purpose is to provide short-term focused help that is effective and appropriate to the workplace culture.

Rogerian counselling

Carl Rogers has been a highly influential thinker in the field of counselling, and a leader in the humanistic category of theoretical models. His main contribution has been in the universal recognition of the three core values – empathy, congruence and unconditional positive regard – that form the bedrock of the counselling approach, whatever theory is overlaid on it. However, when practice is based on the pure principles of Rogerian thought, it tends to be entirely client-led and consequently does not lend itself readily to the short-term focused work required for the workplace.

Cognitive behavioural theory

Cognitive behavioural therapy is a relatively recent development which has had a great deal of success in treating a wide range of emotional disorders, including anxiety and depression, phobias, obsessions and eating disorders. It has its origins in behavioural theory but instead of concentrating on the 'counter-conditioning' of external behaviour, cognitive behavioural therapy addresses itself primarily to the assumptions that lie behind problem behaviour as well as to the behaviour itself.

In the 1960s Professor Aaron Beck of Pennsylvania University applied his new approach mainly to depression. Whereas negative thinking had been thought to be a *symptom* of depression, he proposed that negative thinking patterns laid down in childhood and later, formed the *basis* of depression and also *maintained* it in a kind of vicious circle. He argued against the prevailing view that cast the emotionally disturbed person as 'a victim of concealed forces over which he has no control . . . Man has the key to understanding and solving his psychological disturbance within the scope of his own awareness'. Such was the success of this approach, that cognitive behavioural therapy is now firmly established as a leading therapy in clinical settings.

Treatment takes the form of a very detailed assessment and treatment plan, followed by systematic discussion and behavioural assignments. In this way, clients are helped to recognise, evaluate and modify their own distorted patterns of thinking and functioning.

The cognitive behavioural approach fits well into the organisational world because of its pragmatism, its high success rate, and its short-term emphasis.

Personal construct theory

Personal construct psychology predates cognitive behavioural therapy by about a decade, and is quite similar in its basic propositions. But whereas cognitive behavioural is concerned with the thought itself that leads to a particular behaviour, PCP is more concerned with the dimensions underlying those thoughts – the attitudes, beliefs, prejudices, etc that we bring to our thinking.

George Kelly viewed 'man as scientist': We make sense of our world through a continual process of construing and reconstruing. All of our behaviour is seen as a testing out of our construing, and therefore all behaviour is experimental. We make predictions about the likely outcomes of our actions, based on the hypotheses we hold about the world; we act upon our predictions, and then we adjust our expectations according to whether or not our predictions were accurate. We can never see the world *as it is*. Our construing creates a template of attitudes, beliefs and prejudices through which we view the world; if that template serves us poorly and sets up a process whereby it reinforces itself, then we are in trouble. And a disorder, defined in PCP terms, is any personal construction which is used repeatedly in spite of consistent invalidation.

PCP counsellors use a variety of techniques to gain access to a client's personal world, including the Repertory Grid, and having gained access, try to help the client reconstrue the way in which they view their world.

PCP rejects the notion of the unconscious, and it also fiercely rejects the 'medical model' of disorder. Because of this, PCP has less of a cultural barrier to cross when entering into the organisational context, and is gaining wide acceptance there.

Psychodynamic counselling

'Psychodynamic' is a generic term covering a whole range of theories that share as their pivotal idea the existence of the unconscious mind. Thoughts, feelings and behaviour are all seen as manifestations of drives within the psyche. 'Depth Psychology', as this way of understanding the human mind is also called, began with Freud and was developed by later theorists such as Klein, Winnicott and Bion. They are known as the neo-Freudians, and their specific school of thought is called Psychoanalytic (or Object Relations, in the case of Klein).

Jungian psychology is rather different, though it is also rooted firmly in the unconscious, and it is known as Analytical Psychology. This is a highly complex system of thought, to the extent that it is only ever used at the deeper levels of psychotherapy and analysis. It is never – in our knowlege – used in a systematic way for counselling, nor should it be. Obviously, it would be unsuitable for use in the workplace. For this reason we have not included Jungian psychology in our summary. Interested readers might enjoy *The I and the Not I*, by Esther Harding.[5] The only way in which Jungian theory is applied in organisations, is in the Myers–Briggs® Type Inventory, which is based on Jung's personality types.

From infancy, human beings experience pain and conflict and begin to build defences. We adopt these devices for avoiding the pain and conflict, but the devices are themselves potentially damaging. Bringing the hidden conflicts into consciousness and expressing them is held to be therapeutic, because only by recognising them will we be able to change our life scripts and live more fully. Existential therapists, however, believe that far from being determined by the deep formative influences of our childhoods, we are free at any time to reinvent ourselves according to will.

All depth psychology is complex, and the analytical process can take many years to complete. This, plus its cost and its rootedness in the 'medical model' makes psychoanalysis totally inappropriate in the organisation context. Even psychodynamic counselling tends to be longer term than more cognitively based forms of counselling.

However, psychodynamic theory has some extremely relevant insights to offer the organisational context, both on an individual and group level. For instance, one central idea that informs psychodynamic work is that of 'transference'. This is an unconscious process by which a client displaces on to some other person their attitudes to and feelings for a significant attachment figure of their past. Usually this refers to their relationship with a therapist, but people can just as easily develop a transference to a colleague at work. In this way a manager, say, can find himself at the sharp end of quite inexplicable rage that really belongs at the door of a rival colleague's spoiled older brother. It is usually more subtle than that – and can just as easily be a positive transference as a negative transference.

Group dynamics are also a major concern of the psychoanalytic field. Counsellors whose work is informed by psychodynamic theory will be better equipped to understand many organisational issues, but especially relationships at work.

Most relationship counselling tends to be heavily weighted toward psychodynamic work for exactly this reason.

Transactional analysis

TA (as it is known) is a psychological theory that has found a lot of favour in organisations because its relatively simple, straightforward precepts and methods make it very accessible. It has also proved to be a useful way of looking at how we function as individuals and within relationships.

Eric Berne, who originated transactional analysis, was a trained Freudian analyst and it therefore is not surprising to find a marked similarity to some of Freud's basic ideas. Berne suggested that we function in three different modes, or ego-states (roughly comparable to Freud's id, ego and superego) which he called parent (ego), child (id) and adult (superego). Each of these states has a legitimate part to play in our way of being. The first two can be played out in either positive or negative ways – hence free child and adapted child; nurturing parent and controlling parent. The third, the adult, is used to indicate a state of awareness that reflects all of our positive, grown-up resources. Central to the theory is the notion that we all 'play games'. Games are the devices we learn in childhood to get what we want from the world, but these are mostly outdated and fail to serve us well. As fully aware adults, we are able to employ the full range of options that are open to us. Adult-to-adult relationships are usually the most appropriate to the workplace – and when they are not, trouble often ensues.

TA is a pragmatic and positive way of looking at the human condition that promotes the idea that you do not have to be sick, or even have problems, in order to learn to live more fully. It is currently suffering from having been fashionable, which means that it is now no longer very fashionable in industry. It remains very relevant, however.

Systems theory

This is a framework for understanding the interaction and function of human systems, from marriages and families, to larger organisations. Therapies based on this framework focus attention on the relationship between parts of the group, as opposed to analysis of each separate member of the group. Systems theory has its origins in the work of the biologist Bertalanffy, who described the principles of wholeness, or organisation and the dynamic conception of reality apparent in all fields of science; and it was fed into by developments in the field of cybernetics. Systems theory is essential to the understanding of groups as wholes, rather than as groups of disconnected individual members. The implications of this for teamwork are obvious.

Counsellors working within organisations need not necessarily be systems specialists, because systems theory on its own will not address a wide enough range of the issues that are going to arise. However, they will certainly need a sound working knowledge of systems principles and the ability to think in terms of whole systems, because group dynamics will impinge in some way upon almost every situation in the workplace.

Figure 6
MATRIX OF THEORETICAL MODELS

Model	Workplace useful	Not useful
Rogerian	Creates new relationships based on respect, empathy, genuineness.	Not focused on short-term problem solving. Tends to be entirely client-led; open-ended contract.
Cognitive-behavioural	Focuses on problems and action solutions.	Sometimes fails to address underlying cause – solution may not 'stick'.
Personal construct	Managers relate easily to it – focuses on thinking. Systematic, 'scientific'.	Does not recognise the power of unconscious processes.
Psychodynamic	Relationships, groups, transference – ie unconscious processes.	Focus on long-term development, not short-term problem-solving.
Transactional analysis	As for psychodynamic but more short-term focus.	Not applicable to most non-relationship-based problems.
Systems	Looks at the whole picture – context. Focus on relationship problems.	Does not address individual problems. Useful as adjunct theory but doesn't stand alone without other theories in workplace context.

It can be seen from the matrix (Figure 6) that no theory stands completely alone in the workplace context. We have said previously that because workplace counselling is usually a generalist, rather than a specialist, function counsellors will need to have a broad theoretical and experience base in order to apply themselves to a wide range of demands.

There is one remaining issue that does not fit comfortably into either the skills section, or the theoretical models section. We are referring to neuro-linguistic programming, or NLP, as it has become known. NLP is basically a set of skills rather than a theory or model of understanding, though it has become known as a 'model' in itself. Our purpose in including it, is in order to exclude it from those models we have found useful. This cannot be done by simply ignoring NLP, because it has become a 'fashion'; the issue must be addressed.

Our unease about NLP lies both in its origin and in its application. NLP is not derived from one cohesive theory. It is an amalgam of communication patterns borrowed from the practices of three prominent psychotherapists (Satir, Perls, and hypnotherapist Erikson). In the hands of these expert practitioners they are (or were) effective and safe. However these 'techniques' are abstracted out of the context of experience, theoretical substance, understanding and wisdom whence they came. They are packaged and marketed randomly to anyone who is interested – sales teams are particularly enthusiastic – in whose hands they can become manipulative, and are not necessarily safe. In the literature, words and images like 'trance-formations' and 'frogs into princes' abound, appealing largely to the uninitiated who are attracted by quick-fix solutions. The initiated understand that there are no cures, no ultimate solutions to the human condition. A little knowledge is often a dangerous thing, but it is especially so where people take inappropriate action affecting the well-being of others, believing themselves to be in possession of some kind of magic. We would therefore counsel caution in this regard.

The approach that is needed for counselling and counselling skills in the workplace must be pragmatic, positive and realistic. Ultimately, this is what all counselling is about. Yes, it is there to address conflicts, problems, unhappiness and even unhappiness to the point of sickness. But no, one does not have to be sick in order to benefit substantially from some help sometimes. Even captains of industry have life crises and minor dilemmas. *Everyone* does, and seeking the assistance of an experienced professional, or just a wise friend, in no way implies that the seeker is unable to 'cope'. 'The task of counselling,' the BAC writes, 'is to give the clients an opportunity to explore, discover and clarify ways of living more resourcefully and towards greater well-being.'[6]

References

1. EGAN G. (1986). *The Skilled Helper*. Monteray CA, Brooks Cole, p. 95.
2. *Ibid*. p. 32.
3. *Ibid*. p. 179.
4. SUMMERFIELD J. (1995). Letter published in *Counselling at Work*. BAC Issue No. 7. Winter 1995, p. 14.
5. HARDING E. (1965). *The I and the Not I*. Princeton CA, University of Princeton Press.
6. BAC. *Counselling: Definitions of terms in use, with expansion and rationale*. Rugby, BAC.

Further reading

BANNISTER D. and FRANSELLA F. (1971). *Inquiring Man: The psychology of personal constructs*. London, Routledge.

STEWART I. and JOINES V. (1987). *TA Today*. Nottingham, Lifespace Publishing.

WALROND-SKINNER S. (1986). *Dictionary of Psychotherapy*. London, Routledge & Kegan Paul.

5

WHEN LIFE INTERFERES WITH WORK

A recent article appearing in *The Times* appointments section reported the case of a man who physically assaulted his manager. The man was sacked and subsequently took the company to an industrial tribunal, claiming unfair dismissal. He won the case. The judge's reasons were very clear: he saw it as the manager's responsibility to have known that the man's wife had recently died and that his behaviour was a reaction to his intense feelings of grief.

This case illustrates that there are 'hard' as well as 'soft' reasons why organisations should take note of such cases, a point that we have made before in this book. Because organisations consist of people, there will be times when sad or disturbing life events cannot be left at home. The reactions to these events may not be as extreme as the one illustrated above but, none the less, can result in absenteeism, illness, lack of concentration, increases in mistakes. All of these can badly affect productivity and efficiency.

How to uncover the problems

Of course, some human suffering can be caused by the organisation where, for example, extreme stress results from a variety of causes. In these cases we could be saying the work interferes with life; such stress reactions, and what can be done about them, will be considered in the next chapter.

In this chapter we will look at how human problems can manifest themselves in the workplace. The intention is not to turn people into amateur psychologists, but to help both managers and human resource professionals to recognise where someone might need help and, if necessary, to make a referral (see page 79 in the previous chapter for a rough guide).

Human resource professionals may decide that some of the

problems can be dealt with in-house and might take on the temporary role of counsellor, as mentioned earlier in this book. For example, we could hypothesise that the reason why the man in the tribunal case had such an extreme reaction to his grief could have been due to the idea that he was bottling up his feelings in order to put on a brave face. Many people do not give themselves permission to grieve in this way, especially to colleagues in the workplace, and sometimes need someone to give them permission to do so (more on this shortly). Perhaps if his manager had taken him aside and shown that he recognised that the person was behaving out of character and had enquired if something was wrong, this simple step might have ended with a referral to a trained human resources professional, or externally, rather than in violence and ultimately in an unnecessary cost, not to mention bad publicity, for the organisation.

People, being complex creatures, bring a whole host of issues into the workplace. In this chapter we will look at some of the signs and signals relating to those most commonly encountered. Whether human resource professionals then decide to take on the problem, or to refer outside, will depend on the nature of the problem and their level of skill/training. The point at which a referral could take place will also be discussed.

The authors' view is that the following are the most frequently reported by temporary and full-time counsellors working within organisations: bereavement and loss-type reactions, illness, eating disorders, alcohol and drug abuse, marital and relationship problems, depression and issues associated with age/life stages.

Bereavement and loss

Perhaps one of the most useful realisations about bereavement is the knowledge that it is a process and not a state – a tunnel with an end to it. Counsellors who work mainly with bereaved people will be familiar with William Worden's tasks of mourning.[1] These are:

□   to accept the reality of the loss
□   to experience the pain of grief

☐ to adjust to the new situation
☐ to withdraw emotional energy from the loss and to put it into a new relationship or situation
☐ to integrate the loss.

These tasks can give an illustration of what needs to happen at different stages or phases. Some people experience a period of fantasy where they do not accept the reality of the loss. Extreme cases of people stuck in this phase would be the building of a shrine to the departed or, in the case of redundancy, not believing that it will really happen until the leaving date is upon them.

Experiencing the pain of grief can be problematic for some. If a person has a 'be strong' agenda and is putting on a brave face for the remaining family they may not feel that they can openly express their emotions. These emotions can range from feelings of guilt and sadness to raging anger. Often people in this situation go back to work too soon and their colleagues are either too embarrassed to ask how the person is getting on or afraid of the person breaking down and displaying strong emotions. Our society does not allow for the more cathartic rending of clothes, and weeping and wailing, that takes place in other cultures; the workplace especially is seen as the place where you leave your emotions at home. People may also be afraid of losing their job if they show that they are weak, and there is always the sensitive issue that more may be expected of men in the way of stoicism than of women.

The last two tasks of adjusting to the situation and withdrawing emotional energy take time; however, they are unlikely to happen if the first two tasks have not occurred.

How is all of this likely to manifest itself in the workplace? Certainly, unresolved grief can emerge at some stage in the future, especially if the person experiences another loss. These losses could be as diverse as having your house burgled, losing a treasured object, moving house, breaking a relationship, and, of course, a change of career or a job loss. The idea that people need to go through tasks does imply some action on their part. However, they may need someone to act as a catalyst to bring out the expression of emotion needed for movement through the stages. We could say that never is the talking therapy of counselling more needed for healing than in the case of bereavement.

Signs and signals Where unresolved grief is occurring, ie the person is burying their emotion, the result can be lack of concentration, perhaps resulting in: an increase of errors; bouts of depression; lethargy; inappropriate anger and overreaction (as in the tribunal case mentioned earlier); developing some of the physical symptoms experienced by the deceased just before their death; radical changes in lifestyle which exclude the family, friends or contacts of the deceased; and avoiding talking about or referring to the deceased.

Referral Bereavement is an issue that appropriately trained HR people could handle. What the person wants is the opportunity to ventilate and talk about their feelings. It is important to realise that people will be suffering the effects of grief long after it has ceased to be visible. Often, the time that bereaved people need the most help is after others have forgotten their predicament and withdrawn their support. Referral will be useful when: the HR manager does not have the time to devote to the person; the person is alone and would benefit from being in a contact group of people who have had the same experience; abnormal grief exists. Appendix 1 contains a list of national organisations, the best-known of these being Cruse.

Illness and eating disorders

The outward signs of illness can mean that someone has a condition needing medical attention; however, they could also be indicative of an eating disorder. There are some similarities and some differences. The golden rule is, when in doubt, refer. In other words, it is dangerous to tamper with situations that could be life-threatening to the individual concerned. Where the person's physical appearance has altered eg sudden weight-loss, or even gain (which can be a sign of thyroid deficiency), the first action should be to obtain medical attention as fast as possible.

In the case of terminal illnesses, like cancer or AIDS,

specialist agencies exist which are trained to provide the best possible counselling (see Appendix 1 to this book for a list of national organisations). The reason for eating disorders such as anorexia or bulimia are many and complex and, again, are best dealt with by trained specialists. However, people may not know about these specialists or agencies, and they may be reluctant to seek help until someone in the organisation helps them to give expression to their thoughts and feelings. This may take a few meetings. Once again, managers who come into day-to-day contact with their people should be alert enough to recognise any changes and, if it is not appropriate to spend time with them, refer them to someone who can. The following are some of the less obvious signals that all is not right.

Signs and signals Aside from the more obvious thinness of anorexia and bulimia, signs can include: complaining of persistent stomach pains; swollen fingers (due to excessive use of laxatives); forced vomiting which manifests itself in a puffy face (due to swollen salivary glands); bad teeth (stomach acid dissolves the enamel on the teeth); muscle weakness; and, in some cases, epileptic fits. Anorexics also talk a lot about food, what they will cook, etc., but do not eat it. They may also take vigorous exercise to excess. Bulimics indulge in 'binge' eating but remain thin (owing to vomiting) and both they and anorexics have an abnormal fear of fatness, perceiving themselves much larger and fatter than they actually are. An important point to note is that both anorexics and bulimics become very clever at deception. 'Expert' bulimics learn to vomit discreetly without any visible effects, so the absence of obvious signs in someone who is suspected of being bulimic does not necessarily mean that they are not suffering from this condition.

Referral
As the emotional consequences of both conditions can be depression and loss of concentration, and the physical consequence is death, once again both anorexics and bulimics need specialist help. Any manager or human resources professional suspecting that there is a problem should do all that is in their

power to get the person to a doctor as soon as possible.

Alcohol and drug abuse

According to the CBI, alcohol and drug abuse and the resulting absenteeism, injuries and stealing cost the UK's businesses
billions of pounds each year. The USA has a long history of
tackling alcohol problems, and the original Emzployee
Assistance Programmes, which spawned the UK equivalents,
were founded to try to combat the alcohol problem. Most
large companies have alcohol and drug abuse policies; however, for human resource professionals, the issues of how to
handle people with such problems are complex, and we provide some starting-points.

Alcohol

Drinking alcohol is an acceptable social norm, and most of us
indulge in it from time to time. For some people, however, it
becomes an addiction without which they cannot function.
There is, therefore, a great deal of difference between the
person who takes one or two drinks socially and the person
who has to drink to survive. It is the latter person with whom
we are concerned. They are extremely difficult to detect in the
workplace. There are, however, some tell-tale signs that we
will come to shortly. First of all, a reminder of how alcohol
affects us, and what constitutes normal and abnormal drinking.

Alcohol acts as a depressant on the brain and central nervous system. It works initially on that part of the brain that
controls our inhibitions, so some drinkers become noisy and
boisterous while others become sleepy; it depends on the personality of the individual concerned.

As soon as alcohol enters the bloodstream it begins to affect
judgement, self-control and skills like driving a car or operating heavy machinery. Research has shown that workers who
have drunk between one and three pints of beer have considerably more accidents than those who have drunk less than
one pint of beer. It takes one hour to get rid of one unit of alcohol (a half pint of beer, one glass of wine, one pub measure of
spirit). This means that after a heavy drinking session at

lunchtime someone could still be over the limit in the evening.

Continued excessive drinking, for whatever reason, can lead to dependence. For example, the taking of alcohol to ward off the symptoms of withdrawal is what is meant by alcoholism.

Alcoholics are notoriously difficult to counsel. Characteristically they sabotage any help that you may try to give them because they want to go on drinking. They can make themselves the victim and you the persecutor. It is a disease that, perhaps, only recovering alcoholics really understand; this may be why Alcoholics Anonymous has been so successful in this field.

The authors have experienced such 'games' and recall an alcoholic who was outplaced by their organisation, and who rejected their counsellor as being unsympathetic. He then proceeded to reject every counsellor in the organisation, in turn. This is the typical syndrome of externalising blame. Another sign is that of blaming others for the problem, eg the classic 'I only drink because my wife/husband does not understand me . . .'. Professional counsellors will tell you that, sadly, alcoholics will often ask for help only when they reach rock bottom. Referral is obviously needed and this is where an alcohol policy that promotes disciplinary procedure for persistent drinking at work can be extremely useful. People may be more easily persuaded to seek help if their jobs are at stake.

Signs and signals Heavy drinking can lead to a number of health problems. As alcohol has no nutritional value whatsoever, but many calories, it is possible for a drinker to be overweight and suffering from malnutrition at the same time. If someone is excessively pale, this could be anaemia due to alcohol; a blotchy red skin can be a sign of high blood pressure and toxic reactions to alcohol. General sweatiness is also a symptom.

Alcohol affects judgement and decision-making, so it is logical to suppose that accidents on the shop floor may also be accompanied by bad leadership and ineffective management if there is alcohol abuse at higher levels. Other behaviours include making mistakes, but continuously blaming others (externalising). Another sign is when the person is fine in the morning but changes their mood in the afternoon to an angry, abusive or lethargic one. Watch out for the tell-tale appearance of a jug of 'water' and a glass on the desk: alcoholics will often drink vodka because it is odourless.

In short, any out-of-character behaviour (bouts of temper, dramatic increase of mistakes, inability to meet realistic deadlines) could be attributed to an alcohol problem.

Referral Obviously, alcohol counselling is a complex issue. It is also a very specialised issue. As HR managers are unlikely to have had the special training needed to deal with an alcoholic, referral is essential if an alcohol problem is suspected. The problem is that it is hard to get alcoholics to admit that they have a problem because of the complex characteristics of the illness, some of which we have outlined. Once again, the disciplinary route can be a useful spur in these cases.

Drugs

Here there are some similarities to, and some differences from, alcohol abuse. The similarities are in the manifestation of symptoms and the fact that reformed drug addicts have proved to be the most effective helpers.

The major difference in behaviour is that of stealing in order to maintain an enormously expensive habit. It is reckoned that it costs a full-blown addict £20,000 per year to keep him or her on drugs, and few earners can afford this.

Signs and signals

Drug abuse can be difficult to discern unless an employee is caught stealing company property. Also, different drugs may be more likely to be found in the workplace than others, and they present different symptoms. For example, full-blown heroin addicts are unlikely to be able to hold down a job, whereas the smoking of marijuana may go undetected if not suspected. Cocaine is very expensive and only high-earners will be able to afford it on a regular basis.

Aside from the more obvious spaced-out look, smokers of marijuana have a constantly dry mouth, so may swallow a lot as they talk. Their eyes will be bloodshot and they have difficulty concentrating, and have only short-term memory. A common bad reaction to marijuana is acute panic anxiety reaction, an extreme fear of losing control which shows up as panic. A sign of abuse of cocaine is permanent cold-like symptoms, for example, a blocked or runny nose (chronic 'snorting' can ulcerate the mucous membrane of the nose). The heart rate increases by 50 per cent and may become irregular, causing a heart attack, or even cardiac arrest. In some cases brain seizures occur, causing an epileptic seizure. Other less obvious signs include: dilated pupils; lung disorders; bronchitis; a chronic cough; hoarseness and wheezing. The well-publicised drug ecstasy also causes similar cold-like symptoms and is more prevalent in younger abusers, who may just now be coming onto the job market.

Heroin abusers may still be working during the early days of their habit and for them the major sign would be constant fluctuations between being alert and drowsy. With larger doses the user becomes extremely drowsy; the pupils become small; the user may fall into a sleep from which they cannot be awoken; the skin becomes cold, moist and bluish; breathing slows down and death can occur.

A major symptom with all addicts is that they do not eat or sleep properly (as with alcohol), so sudden and prolonged weight loss and exhaustion from any physical exercise will occur. As mentioned earlier, it seems unlikely that a full-blown addict will still be able to function at work. One could argue that this is also the case with alcoholics, although the social unacceptability of drugs, compared with alcohol, may work to the addict's advantage. It is more likely to be accepted as a problem and people may be more motivated to offer help.

Referral
A health warning for would-be counsellors; look for uncharacteristic changes that may be similar to the ones we have described, but don't feel pressurised into thinking that you are the best person to counsel. Alcoholics Anonymous are also a good port of call in the case of drugs, and may refer to other organisations such as 'Narconon' which has had great success in this area. Narconon employs a technique called the 'Minnesota System', the success of which demonstrated that education and counselling alone were not effective in

combating the problem. The system involves training former addicts to help others, education of the public and children in particular, purification techniques which rid the body of toxins as a remedy for existing cases and counselling to prevent reversion to the old habit. Clearly, as with alcohol, drug abuse is a complex issue and is best left to the experts.

Marriage and relationships

The central relationships in our lives, particularly marriage and other long-term committed partnerships, are so pivotal to our general stability and well-being that when they go wrong, relationships and performance at work will almost certainly both be affected. People prefer, by and large, to keep their personal and working lives separate, and because marital problems can be so beset by denial anyway, marital dysfunction as a root cause of poor professional performance can lie undetected for years – even decades. Even when there are strong indications that someone may be silently suffering in this way, the intensely personal nature of the subject makes it difficult to approach. The line between intrusion and valid concern is so fine as to be imperceptible. When a marriage finally reaches the point of divorce – or any couple-relationship reaches the point of final breakdown – the matter usually becomes public, and colleagues may then feel free to express support. But by then – from the marriage (or relationship) point of view – it is too late.

Counselling agencies like Relate and London Marriage Guidance have come under heavy criticism in the media lately for failing to mend marriages that are in fact beyond repair. What the critics – many of whom should have known better – have failed to understand is the critical element of timing. All too often fear, denial and conflicting agendas conspire to keep couples from seeking help until they are in crisis. And all too often, that is too late. Those who are genuinely concerned to protect the institution of marriage would do better to encourage couples to seek help earlier, rather than discourage them from seeking it at all. The HR or line manager possibly has a role to play here, if the problem is apparent. A gentle nudging in the direction of professional help might encourage the person to take counselling. People are often reluctant to seek help for various reasons, some of which are pure misapprehension. We will briefly outline some of the commonest barriers.

'*Just me*'. This one takes many forms: 'My spouse seems happy enough with the marriage, perhaps it's just me.'

Or, 'My spouse/partner says I'm the one with the problem,'

Or, indeed, 'I'm not the one with the problem, it's her/him.'

Or, 'If I just try a little harder/just do this/just do that/wait a bit longer, etc. the problem will go away.' (It may, for a while, but the chances are it will soon be back, and worse.)

These are all examples of avoidance or denial. Anything, even the pain, is better than confronting the reality. One of the real problems of being within a long-term relationship is the lack of an external reference point. Often the only other marriage we may have known from close-up is that of our parents and, it turns out, they were human too. How then do we measure our experience of intimate relationship in the comparative way we measure and make sense of other facets of our lives? How 'unhappy' is 'too unhappy', and how happy are we *supposed* to be? Often people have been unhappy for so long they have forgotten how 'happy' feels. The problem is compounded by the fact that two people's experience of the same marriage can be so different. This may only mean that one person has everything their way, at the expense of the other – but the discrepancy is confusing in itself, to both partners. In this way we mistrust our own instincts, and fail to act upon them in a constructive way.

Even when couples have found the courage to seek help, avoidance or denial can subvert the helping process. Some will stick with the process and 'tough it out', and when that happens, the prognosis for the marriage is good; but it is not unknown for one or both partners to take flight from counselling when painful truths loom perilously close. Sometimes they will give up in anger or despair, but just as often they will take a 'flight into health'. This is the professional term for postponing a problem, or sweeping it back under the carpet.

The important thing to remember in the 'just me' scenario is that a relationship is two people. If one of those people thinks that something is wrong, then by definition, it is. And that, in itself, is a good enough reason for both to seek help. This situation often leads to the following common misconception.

'*My spouse refuses to seek help, so we cannot benefit from counselling.*' Spouses who refuse to go into counselling at their husband's or wife's request will very often respond positively to a written invitation from the counsellor. However, if one partner persists in refusing to co-operate, or if the other is for whatever reason too reticent to ask the partner to attend, it is possible to go alone. The person who refuses will often have a vested interest in keeping the *status quo* exactly as it is, possibly without even knowing why. This kind of resistance is most usefully explored by the couple together. But if that position is not held by common consent, there is a lot that one partner can do to shift the balance. When one half of a couple begins to grow and change, this has a ripple effect on the whole pattern of couple dynamics. The result may be to make it easier to conduct the relationship in a more satisfying way.

It has to be said, though, that an enabled person will sometimes feel enabled to leave the partnership! Counselling cannot make someone go back who has decided to leave, and that is not its purpose. In such cases, helping a couple to end a relationship with a minimum of acrimony will be seen as a successful outcome.

'*The waiting lists are too long.*' This is a problem for the agencies as well as for those seeking help from them. When the need arises it is usually urgent, and by the time the opportunity arises the crisis has passed. Most counsellors at the agencies prefer to work social hours, like everyone else, and that means there is often a dearth of free appointments at precisely the times they are needed most. Here the organisation can be helpful in granting time out for counselling during working hours. Between nine and five the waiting lists are often dramatically shorter.

Signs and signals

The signs that someone is suffering from domestic conflict may be the same as for more generalised distress, namely poor concentration, poor performance, low energy or exhaustion, perhaps irritability, and so on. These may also be quite erratic, as better or worse phases at home set the tone for behaviour at work. Because of the deeply personal nature of the cause, it may only emerge in the context of performance management counselling. (See Referral section, below.) Although many people will be reticent about discussing the cause of their distress, there may be other ways in which they will signal the need for help: increased drinking; dismissive or critical comments about their spouse; a tendency to make inappropriate relationships at the office; and 'workaholism' – as a way of avoiding returning home. Sometimes it can work the other way. An obsession with work, or a work culture that makes unreasonable demands, can create the marital conflict. Any apparent advantage of this to the organisation will be short term, as performance is eventually eroded. Either way there is a problem to be addressed.

One or more of these patterns, observed over a period of time, could provide an opportunity to make a tentative enquiry. Some people may exhibit quite extravagant signs, but for others the signs will be subtle and easily missed. When the divorce (or final breakdown) stage of a relationship is reached, the distress is greatly intensified. The way that divorce legislation has been structured, this period could last two years or more, with the times following the separation and preceding the 'petitioning' being particularly chaotic. New no-fault divorce law looks set to reduce considerably the burden of bitterness on divorcing couples. However, the pain of loss – of the relationship, children, financial security, friends, status and self-esteem – will remain. It should be noted that mediation serves a different purpose from that of marital counselling: if a couple is wavering, mediation could be a route back into counselling. But at this stage of marital breakdown, though a counsellor is present at mediation, the emphasis will normally be on settlement of financial and child-related disputes prior to divorce.

Referral
Marital therapy is a specialised form of counselling. If the need for it becomes clear, an employee can be referred directly

to an external agency such as Relate, or to an internal counsellor if he or she has specialist relationship training. It is quite possible that, where the signs have been well disguised, the employee may be in general counselling – perhaps for poor performance – before the marital problems emerge as a cause. There will need to be a clear policy of referral on to a specialist counsellor in such cases. Marital/relationship difficulties form a large part of EAP work. A general culture of availability and acceptability of counselling is important in allowing people to bring these problems to the surface.

Depression

One of the effects of long-term stress is depression but there are other causes for a depressive reaction and reactive depression, which are common reactions to loss and unhappy life-events. A depressive reaction (sadness, to you and me) is not the same as reactive depression – but it is largely a matter of degree. The former is a transient state of sadness, and counselling in the workplace by a trained person can help a great deal as the causes are uncovered and aired.

Reactive depression is more serious. It is longer term and more severe, but will usually respond to professional counselling. The sufferer's general practitioner should be the first port of call. When people hit a major bad life-event, or even a series of small ones that build up, they can become depressed. Most people do not realise that this is a normal reaction to abnormal events, and often feel guilty about being depressed, which all adds to the general misery. It should be noted that reactive depression can slip into depressive illness, or endogenous depression (which means, literally, 'coming from within'). Normally, though, endogenous depression seems to come 'out of the blue', for no apparent reason. It is the most severe form of depression, and sufferers will find it extremely difficult to function at work – unlike the reactively depressed person who may lose concentration only temporarily. They cannot make decisions, and dither endlessly.

People with this sort of depression often have a chemical imbalance in their bodies which will respond well to treatment if correctly diagnosed. Anti-depressants can be useful to help a person through a bad phase, and counselling will provide support and alleviate the guilt feelings. Counselling, either on its own or with anti-depressants, will offer the person an opportunity to find the strength and confidence to handle the problem. People tend to get anti-depressants confused with tranquillisers, and so refuse them for fear of becoming chemically dependent. The two have a completely different action and purpose. Most importantly, anti-depressants are *not* addictive, and can be life-savers. Depressed people should be encouraged to discuss this further with their general practitioners. In the most serious cases, a combination of anti-depressants in tandem with cognitive behavioural therapy has proved to be the most effective.

The difference between the two kinds of depression is not always clear. Most symptoms refer to both conditions, and it is only when someone begins to counsel that the differences may become more apparent. For most, the reassurance that comes from counselling that they are not going mad can bring some immediate relief. Most people have a horror of mental illness and may, indeed, think that they are ill when they are not. One risk for people with depressive illness is that if they are dismissed for odd behaviour, their doctor might think it is a reactive depression due to job loss, and miss the illness. This makes the task of getting them into counselling all the more urgent.

Ironically, the most seriously depressed person is at less risk of suicide than the more moderately depressed. In the depths of the deepest depression, there is not even the energy for suicide. Do not imagine, therefore, that because someone is less seriously depressed that they are not at risk.

Signs and Signals
Sadness, disturbance of sleep, and disturbance of appetite are three of the most common symptoms. If a person complains of early waking (3 or 4 am) every night, combined with an inability to get back to sleep, this is likely to be a sign of depression – although overstressed people do the same thing. The person is generally downbeat and nothing gives them pleasure or seems fun any more. Other symptoms include self-neglect, loss of self-confidence (particularly in endogenous

depression), poor memory, suicidal thoughts, agitation and anxiety, loss of sexual appetite. Differences between the two types are said to be that endogenously depressed people go off their food, while reactives often eat more; the endogenous group awake early in the morning and the reactives have difficulty falling asleep, yet wake at the normal time after a fitful night's sleep.

There are two other forms of depression that should be mentioned briefly, because these may be found quite regularly in organisations, for different reasons.

Masked depression is a form that manifests itself entirely as physical symptoms. These can include headaches, nausea, shakiness, dizziness, blurred vision, constipation or diarrhoea, difficulty with breathing, a sense of food 'sticking' at the top of the stomach, excessive sweating, pains, or other symptoms. Eventually sufferers become regarded as hypochondriacs. It is easy to see how a highly competitive culture could lead to the unconscious masking of depression, though this is not proven to be the cause. Ironically, if it is not diagnosed and properly treated early enough, the sufferer becomes quite disabled socially.

Manic depression is a form of endogenous depression characterised by extreme swings of mood. This dramatic pattern of great highs followed by a crash into profound lows, occurs in cycles of between six months and five years. The condition has been proved to be genetically inherited and is extremely dangerous to the sufferer, but can be effectively treated. These are frequently highly talented and charismatic people, so they will often be very successful. Many who do not complain to their doctors of depression 'will show up with family or social problems such as shoplifting, traffic offences, marital breakdowns, heavy drinking or failure at important tasks in life. If these crises were handled in the normal way and the underlying diagnosis missed, the patient would lose out and might commit suicide.'[2]

Referral It is important to note that most people have highs and lows. The sort we have described are extreme. Nevertheless it is important to check out worrying symptoms, because getting someone to the right help in time could literally save a life. There is still much disagreement in medical circles about how the two major types of depression overlap. Trained HR professionals have a vital role to play. Very often, sadness can be effectively dealt with at a first-stage skills level by a trained HR professional, preventing further distress. If there is any doubt at all about the nature of the depression, it is vital that the person be referred to their GP. It is very important that HR people are alert to the general patterns of symptoms and feel able to make appropriate moves toward someone they are becoming concerned about. It is not a 'diagnosis' that is called for but an early-warning signal.

Age and life stages

Most people in the workplace fall into two life stage categories: early adulthood (20 to 40 years) and mid-life (40 to 60 years). For each of these groups the life issues are different, although many events such as bereavement and separation can, of course, occur at either stage.

People in the early adult stage may experience a variety of things that affect the way they are at work. For example, they may lack confidence for a variety of social situations. Certainly they will be absorbed more with their social life and things like choosing a partner or finding a place to live. They may not have yet found their way in their career and will more easily hop from job to job than those in the mid-life phase.(This rather makes a nonsense of ageism, where older, more experienced and potentially more stable people are rejected as potential candidates for jobs.) Younger people can also be subject to bullying by older managers and may lack the confidence and wherewithal to try to sort this out. Such situations will almost certainly block originality and creativity in an organisation nurturing its future resources. In these situations the human resources manager, being removed from the line, may be the only person to whom the individual can turn, and who is in a position to confront the bully.

Young men, having taken on commitments, often find themselves with conflicting demands of family and career growth. This can lead to marital difficulties. For women with young families, the issues can be around balancing home and work demands. In recent years women have shown a sharp increase in their likelihood to develop heart disease and stress symptoms in the workplace. Although the 'glass ceiling' undoubtedly exists (in itself a form of stress), more women are winning middle management positions, and organisational counsellors often report a kind of female macho-ness or the superwoman syndrome, where women feel that they have to be the perfect wife, mother and career woman; as a consequence they put themselves under enormous pressure.

In mid-life both men and women can experience what has become known as the mid-life crisis. A combination of situations can come together to cause this, including:

☐ the empty-nest syndrome, where children have grown up and gone to university or have made their own homes. If the relationship is weak, or has been faltering, having to be more focused on each other can often prove the breaking-point for some couples.

☐ health and fitness. For women, the onset of the menopause means the end of child-bearing years and this can depress older women who have not had children. Also, the symptoms are subtle and can creep up on women who, suffering from abnormal tiredness, mood swings, disturbed sleep patterns, night sweats, hot flushes and skin problems may not recognise these as the signs of the menopause. This is exacerbated by the fact that many GPs do not recognise them either, in one case wrongly diagnosing the symptoms as stress and anxiety, and putting the woman on anti-depressants.

For men the issues around ageing can be to do with the realisation that they have not progressed far enough up the ladder in their careers. As senior management is still commonly agreed to be a sign of success, they may need career counselling to re-evaluate their aspirations. There is also the much sensationalised need that some men have to prove that they are still sexually potent by attracting younger women. Those HR managers who have had to untangle a knotty and destructive sexual intrigue in the office will know that the height of diplomacy, as well as a cast-iron commitment to confidentiality, is needed.

☐ bereavement and loss. As people grow older they also experience the loss of parents and close relatives, or may have the responsibility for looking after a sick parent. For both men and women this, combined with children leaving home, and in some cases redundancy, can flip them into depression.

Signs and signals In some ways we come full circle to the story of the man who had lost his wife that we told at the beginning of this chapter. Managers, noticing changes in behaviour, increase of mistakes and decrease of performance generally should be aware of the human and legal consequences of the disciplinary route being their first port of call. HR managers can play a vital role here in training managers to be aware of the signs and signals and to use basic counselling skills when they approach the person.

Referral In any situation where there may be a possible health problem HR managers must encourage the person to seek medical advice. Where they can play a vital role is in staying with the person to support them and in suggesting further action if that advice does not sort out the problem. People who are ill can lose the confidence that comes with good health and may not have the wherewithal to press for better treatment.

The internal HR professional, acting temporarily as counsellor, can do a great deal of good to resolve many of the problems we have considered in this chapter. People are unlikely to seek outside help from counsellors who will have no influence to change the situation in the workplace. Also, general fear and misunderstanding about counselling still prevails: 'It is for people with mental problems isn't it?' Seeking a counsellor could be viewed by some as an admission of failure.

As we have said before in this book, the HR manager, trained and aware, will play a vital role in bridging the worlds of work and of counselling, making the one accessible to the other.

Life interferes with work . . but the one need not destroy the other.

References

1. WORDEN W. (1992). *Grief Counselling and Grief Therapy.* London, Tavistock Press.
2. STANWAY A. (1981). *Overcoming Depression.* London, Hamlyn.

Further reading

BUCKROYD J. (1989). *Eating Your Heart Out: The emotional meaning of eating disorders.* MacDonald Optima.

ECKERSLEY K. (1993). 'Danger: drugs at work. Why counselling comes last.' *Employee Counselling Today.* Vol. 15, pp. 7–11.

FISHER M. and WARMAN J. (1990). *Bereavement and Loss: A skills companion.* Cambridge, National Extension College.

LEVINSON D. J. (1978). *The Seasons of a Man's Life.* New York, Alfred A. Knopf Inc.

MURRAY THOMAS R. (1990). *Counselling and Life Span Development.* London, Sage.

POST OFFICE VIDEO SERVICES. (1985). *Someone Like You.*

TATELBAUM J. (1980). *The Courage to Grieve.* London, Heinemann.

VELLEMAN R. (1989). 'Counselling people with alcohol and drug problems.' In W. Dryden, D. Charles-Edwards and R. Woolfe (eds), *Handbook of Counselling in Britain.* London, Tavistock Press.

6

WHEN WORK INTERFERES
WITH LIFE

The focus of this chapter is occupational stress. What is it, and how can employers help people to manage it? Everyone has some knowledge of stress, because everyone has experienced it. We are all familiar with the racing pulse, the sweaty palms, the constricted throat and a host of other unpleasant sensations that we associate with stress reaction.

The long-term consequences of stress are dire. For the individual, effects can include damage to the cardiovascular system; depletion of the immune system, with resulting susceptibility to infection and tumour growth; sleep disturbance and chronic tiredness; ulcers, digestive tract disease and muscular disorders – and those are just the physiological dangers. For the organisation, the effects of individual stress on corporate functioning are profound.[1]

'Don't tell me to relax,' the joke goes. 'It's only my tension that's holding me together.' The serious point is that we all need a *degree* of stress. Hans Selye, the Canadian endocrinologist who developed the concept of stress, drew a distinction between positive stress – the sort that gives life its excitement, challenge and edge – and the harmful sort, that we experience as distress. Degree is the operative word. How much is too much? The answer is: it depends.

Each of us experiences stress in a very individual way. We react to different triggers, produce different symptoms, respond with different coping strategies, and recover at different rates. The optimum balance of challenge and coping resources differs widely between individuals.

Down in the ladies' lavatories at Paddington Station there was, for many years, a wonderful woman who called everyone 'my darling' and sang praises to The Lord at the top of her voice from the beginning of her shift to the end. She was a joy to all who passed her way, and few who entered left without a smile and a better start to their day.

'Right livelihood', the Buddha taught, is part of the Noble Eightfold Path that leads to enlightenment. It is work that does not hurt anyone because, the wisdom goes, it is not possible to be happy while in the process of undoing others' happiness. In the corporate life of the 1990s, stress and the unhappiness it causes – to both the sufferer and those around him – is part of the reality of daily life.

'Wrong livelihood' is so endemic and creates such enormous stress that it claims lives, and creates livelihoods for researchers, medics and organisation consultants. By 'wrong livelihood' we do not simply mean being in the wrong job. We also mean working in an organisational environment or culture which fails to permit personal satisfaction and productivity. The delicate balance between talent, realism, opportunity, and will is easily upset, and when we are disconnected from our talents, they suddenly pop up as needs. What is right for some may be quite wrong for others. How can a culture be created that nurtures such a wide range of personalities? By definition, it is a culture in which individuals are valued for their particular contributions, and are helped to overcome obstacles to satisfaction and productivity.

Often when an organisation goes shopping for an EAP, it is attracted to those that lay heavy emphasis on employees' personal problems – family benefits, 24-hour helplines and the like. Since work is what we do with most of our waking lives, many of life's problems either have their origins in the workplace or are exacerbated by workplace demands. Because the workplace ethos is one that demands a high degree of competitiveness, the only place to take worries is home – and there they certainly will have an impact on personal lives. Of course, addressing home concerns will also bring benefits to work performance, but it is *right here inside the workplace*, we suggest, that the real core of an employer's responsibilities lie.

We emphasise this because the choice of counselling resource is so crucially important. How can a counselling service that addresses only personal problems, or addresses work-related problems without any relation to the embedding culture, meet that core responsibility?

In this chapter we look at stress itself, at some of the ways in which corporate life can cause stress, and how stress manifests itself in the workplace. The following specific issues will be discussed: difficult working relationships; bullying and disciplinary counselling; survivor syndrome; post-traumatic stress; and critical incident debriefing. In the Further Reading section at the end of this chapter we will suggest publications of interest, and agencies for referral onward are listed in Appendix 1. (Career counselling is discussed in Chapter 8.)

What is stress?

Stress is defined as occurring when there is an imbalance between the demands of the environment and the resources we have to meet them.

There have been several models of stress over the years. Selye's original work in the 1950s defined a pattern of adaptation (alarm, resistance and collapse) over the course of prolonged exposure to stress. His view was challenged on two accounts: first, it did not take sufficiently into account the differences between individuals, and, secondly, it assumed the same pattern of response for different kinds of stressors. In the late 1960s, Holmes and Rahe identified 43 stressful life events, to which they assigned points on their 'social readjustment rating scale'. So divorce, for instance, scored 73, and going on holiday, 13. It was the accumulation of such changes, they observed, that caused stress. This idea addressed the differential pattern of external events, but failed to acknowledge the individual nature of response.

Perhaps the most helpful way of looking at stress thus far has been through the transactional (or interactional) model. Researchers Lazarus and Folkman[2] proposed this model which has found favour because it takes into account the two-way process that 'winds us up'. Stress approaches, as it were, from two directions – from our environment (external factors), and from our internal responses. This model emphasises the ongoing nature of the balance or imbalance. It also recognises that not only do environments influence people, but people influence their environments.

The implication of this for the organisation is that it, too, needs to approach the problem from two directions:

☐ First, it needs to recognise and address the stressors within the organisation. Counselling is one important way of locating the stressors. Addressing them is done in several ways: policy is the corporate way; education and training programmes are the HR way; and practical approaches (such as, for instance, security systems) are the operational way.

☐ Secondly, affected employees will need help on an individual level through counselling, stress profiling and perhaps relaxation training.

External factors

These fall into two broad categories: acute and chronic. Acute are the 'sledgehammer' stresses. They are the major blows: redundancy/outplacement; violent attack; and other one-off crises. Chronic stress, or prolonged duress, is the repetitive, low-level variety created by a combination of day-to-day stressors within the organisation: overemployment or underemployment; the demands of corporate culture on individuals, including survivor syndrome; relationship, political and career disturbances. We will look in greater detail at three examples in the following section.

Internal responses

It was an upholsterer who first noticed the connection between personality type and coronary heart disease. There was a curious pattern of wear on the front edges of the chairs at the unit at Mount Zion Hospital in San Francisco, where cardiologists Friedman and Rosenman were conducting their research; in particular, they were looking at the way a person's feelings or thoughts might influence development of the disease. But the upholsterer's observation was not heeded.

Some time later (in 1956) a detailed diet survey revealed that diet and smoking alone could not account for the seemingly erratic patterns of cholesterol metabolism across different population groups. But one of Friedman's research subjects thought she knew the answer. 'If you really want to know what is going to give our husbands heart attacks, I'll tell you,' she said. 'It's stress – the stress they have to face in their businesses, day in, day out. Why, when my husband comes home at night, it takes at least one martini just to unclench his jaws.' Friedman and Rosenman had been growing increasingly suspicious about the possible role of emotional stress, and this was all the encouragement they needed. Intensive research into this connection provided overwhelming confirmation, and in the *Journal of the American Medical Association* in 1959, the concept of Type A and Type B behaviour was officially born.

Friedman and Ulmer,[3] describe Type A behaviour as

> above all a continuous struggle, an unremitting attempt to accomplish or achieve more and more things or participate in more and more events in less and less time, frequently in the face of opposition – real or imagined – from other persons. The Type A personality is dominated by covert *insecurity of status or hyper-aggressiveness*, or both.
>
> It is one or both of these two basic components that generally causes the struggle to begin. The struggle itself sooner or later fosters the emergence of a third personality ingredient, that *sense of time urgency* we have designated hurry sickness. As the struggle continues, the hyper-aggressiveness (and also perhaps the status insecurity) usually shows itself in the easily aroused anger we term *free-floating hostility*. Finally, if the struggle becomes severe enough and persists long enough, it may lead to a fifth component: a tendency toward *self-destruction*.

Type As find it difficult, if not impossible, to acknowledge that a more relaxed way of approaching life is at least as likely to lead to success, or even greatness; Type As only tend to be more conspicuous in that role. Their obsessive drive to succeed often does lead to success. It also leads ultimately to destruction – not only of self, but of others, relationships, entire corporations – and even countries. Such people leave trails of devastation in their wake.

Since its implication in the development of heart disease has been discovered, stress has also been implicated in the horrific catalogue of disorders we mentioned at the beginning of this chapter. When the idea of Type A and Type B behaviour first entered the public domain, type-spotting became a popular parlour game. But type-spotters invariably found it easier to spot Type A behaviour in others than in themselves.

Recognising the pattern is one thing; treating it is another. The good news is that there is a great deal that can be done. The same researchers who discovered Type A behaviour conducted a four-year study aimed at discovering whether it was possible to modify this condition, and whether doing so would actually reduce the risk of heart attack. All of the 1,000 participants had had at least one heart attack, and all received special Type A counselling. Not only did most of the participants succeed in changing their behaviour patterns, they also cut their heart-attack rate by half when measured against statistical expectation. One group achieved a 75 per cent reduction.

There are, of course, more than two kinds of people, and therefore there are other variables in the treatment of stress. Some physical types, for instance, will reduce stress levels dramatically by taking physical exercise; others will not benefit at all.

The importance of individuality is difficult to overstate. The beauty of successful stress counselling though, is that it not only transforms the life of the sufferer himself, it dramatically reduces the burden of stress on all around him.

Workplace bullying

Whereas it is quite true that bullies do not need any external provocation to activate their behaviour, it is also true that high levels of stress in the organisation will aggravate it considerably. Dealing with stress by dumping it on others is a common phenomenon.

Because all but the most exceptional of organisations have their own liberal sprinkling of Type As, the chances are that anyone reading the description above will have recognised particular people. The further chances are that those people will be causing untold damage not only to themselves but to their subordinates and also to the organisation. Unless their victims have the courage to complain (which often they do not) or someone else in authority is particularly astute, they may remain undetected. This is because it is likely that they will be charm itself to anyone over whom they do not exercise control, and may even be promoted to positions that will enable them to broaden their sphere of bullying activities. They may be efficient and even talented in their professional capacities. However, the hidden costs of their pernicious behaviour, in terms of absenteeism and the devastation of competence of those affected by them, are grossly disproportionate to the benefits. Professor Cary Cooper of UMIST has estimated that bullying is the direct cause of between a third and a half of all stress-related illness at work, a figure the CBI puts at between £1 billion and £2 billion a year. Of course, the ideal solution is to lose neither the talents of the bully nor those of his colleagues.

There is legislation against some forms of discrimination, notably race and sex. Some unions are pushing for legislation such as that passed in Sweden last year, making harassment an offence. But harassment and in particular some forms of abuse – ostracism, continuous destructive criticism, verbal abuse and the like – can be very subtle and therefore difficult to prove and combat. Complaints and disciplinary procedures are a necessary, but only partially effective, solution to the problem. A small minority of organisations is addressing harassment at a policy level, but in itself that is not enough. It is also very important to provide an environment where people feel able to air their complaints and to do so with confidence that they will be taken seriously.

We know from playgrounds that bullying, undealt with, becomes worse. The victim hopes the opposite: that if he keeps his head down or tries harder the problem will go away. The bully, who is himself deeply inadequate, is affirmed by this submission. Thus the destructive cycle is maintained. Although it is necessary to prevent the persecutor from wreaking his havoc this does not address the root of the problem. Nor does rescuing the victim. The underlying dynamic maintaining that *status quo* must be reversed if the persecutor is not to find another victim – and vice versa.

Transactional analysis has a model that is very pertinent to this situation. Called the drama triangle, it proposes that the persecutor, victim and rescuer are all players in the same neurotic game. Each has a set of faulty assumptions about himself in relation to others, and a hidden agenda. These need to be explored and firmly challenged before that pattern can be changed. A general point about counselling relationships at work is that in some ways it is not dissimilar to marital counselling. There are not the same conflicts about intimacy or, say, commitment, but all the same power struggles and transferences come into play.

Signs and signals Look for team conflicts, or the 'odd person out'; timidity, tearfulness or low self-confidence. Performance problems, especially uncharacteristically high levels of error, could point to bullying, but also to other sources of distress.

What the manager/HR professional can do
Dealing with the immediate situation is important.

☐ Listen to, and take seriously, this kind of complaint. Remember it will not have been easy for the victim to seek assistance. Even though the complaints may sound trivial, that is not the way they will have been experienced. Anyone who has ever been on the receiving end will know how brutal this kind of systematic undermining is. If there is cause to doubt the veracity of the statement, it may be thought appropriate to do some 'reality testing' in the form of dyadic or triadic questioning (see page 44).

☐ It may be helpful to approach someone if there is enough evidence to suggest they may be suffering: 'I have been concerned about you recently because I have noticed that (mention a specific behaviour or generalised concern). Is something troubling you?/ Is there anything you would like to talk about?' etc.

☐ There may be sufficient evidence to issue a warning or begin a complaints or disciplinary procedure immediately, but if not, encourage the victim to keep a journal of specific incidents and feelings.

Referral Managing the immediate situation will need backing up with some counselling support if it is to be prevented from recurring. Depending on the complexity of the underlying assumptions, a skills-trained HR or management professional may or may not be able to counsel both parties to the situation. The victim will need time and a safe place to offload some of the *angst* he has absorbed. He may also need help with assertiveness, and for some this is much more difficult than for others. For the persecutor, counselling should go hand-in-hand with disciplinary procedures and, again, this will be more difficult for some than for others. Some may not be amenable to help at all. These are judgments that need to be made on a case-by-case basis. As with all relationship counselling, care will need to be taken to avoid colluding with one or other of the parties. One last thing to remember is the differential response we discussed earlier. What is tolerable for one may be overwhelming for another. Therefore what feels like bullying to the second may seem like simple insensitivity to the first. Either way it is important to address, and to maintain an even-handed approach.

Sexual and racial harassment

The important thing to remember about sexual and racial harassment is that both are forms of bullying. This is sometimes hard to see in the case of sexual harassment, because it may not necessarily appear to be aggressive. However, whether the bullying is overt or not, what is really happening is that the persecutor is playing some kind of power game. The main difference between dealing with 'unspecific' bullying and bullying that involves a racial or sexual element is that the latter is illegal. This means that the human resource professional will need to consult an employment law handbook rather than a counselling handbook, at least until the matter is legally concluded. When the legalities have been dealt with, some counselling may still be necessary and, if so, treat the issue as for bullying.

Survivor syndrome

When the big shakedown first began in the 1980s – de-layering, downsizing, rightsizing, re-engineering, call it what you will – organisations were largely aware of the need to take a constructive approach to redundancy, and outplacement became the new growth industry. What employers found they had not anticipated, however, was the strange kind of malaise afflicting those who were fortunate enough to remain. Some of those responses looked remarkably like mourning: shock and disbelief, guilt and anger, sadness and resentment. These reactions led to a decrease in motivation and loyalty to the organisation, increased stress levels and a much heightened sense of insecurity, with a corresponding withdrawal of commitment. The recognisable pattern was so widespread that the term *survivor syndrome* was coined.

Change management has since become an area of specialist skill in itself. Innovative organisations have adopted a wide variety of creative ways to reduce the impact of change programmes and rebuild staff morale. Birmingham Midshires Building Society took managers off-site for additional skills training before their planned announcement; a helpline and professional counselling support were provided for the most emotional period; the executive team visited each location over a period of eight weeks to answer employees' concerns and questions about their future; an outplacement facility was established in separate offices with a communication link to inform staff how their former colleagues were progressing in the job market; a personal development planning process was launched, giving all staff a minimum of six days' training for the year; a financial incentive plan was put in place to reward employees for increased profitability and customer satisfaction. Staff attitude surveys were carried out annually. These indicated a high level of acceptance and adjustment to the new culture right across the business, says Lorren Wyatt, BMBS's director of human resources.

Recently the surveys were developed into a continuous monitoring of staff attitudes that closely parallels BMBS's customer satisfaction research. By a process that is both simple and highly original, staff feedback is given daily and measured on a monthly basis. The results so far are encouraging. There appears to be a high correlation between staff attitude and customer satisfaction – and since the Society has won awards for customer satisfaction, this suggests that, from an employee point of view, the change strategy has been very successful too.

The results demonstrate the value of taking an integrated approach to a large-scale problem, one which combines preventive measures with the strategic use of counselling. Looking at the initiatives listed above, it can be seen that there are three core elements to successful change:

- [ ] There is heavy emphasis on open, honest and timely communication to counter insecurity.
- [ ] There is counselling support to deal with the emotional impact of loss and disorientation.
- [ ] Personal/career development planning is made for adjustment to the new realities.

Counselling and counselling skills have a major contribution to make in each area.

The communication style necessary for this task is as much about listening skilfully as it is about giving information. The value of this process is self-evident, because uncertainty is the most fertile breeding-ground for rumour, and rumour feeds insecurity and anger at an alarming pace. Information must not only be reliable: it must be responsive, as far as possible, to the perceptions of those affected. This implies also that enough allowance must be made for correcting errors in the process without compromising the overall plan. The manner in which this exchange is conducted is vital in establishing the trust necessary to moving forward on a sure footing. Research carried out into the reactions of survivors of layoffs,[4,5] found that the most important factor in how employees feel is whether they see the behaviour of management as fair. In smoothing the course of change, there are no substitutes for good planning, good timing and honest communication, sensitively handled.

Outplacement counselling is essential for the leavers. For the survivors, its provision is evidence of fairness and caring on the part of the organisation. But direct counselling for the survivors will be necessary also. We have referred to the similarities – in process, if not intensity – between bereavement loss and survivor loss. Close friends are often amongst the casualties. Coupled with the grief that is felt on their behalf, there is the survivor's own sense of loss. The guilt is a double-edged sword:

not only is there guilt about surviving, there is guilt about feeling relief about surviving.

Whenever we are faced with change, whether positive or negative, its bright side is the opportunity for renewal. The shadow side is fear. When that fear hooks into one of our most primitive drives, like the need to provide for ourselves and our families, the resulting anxiety can be debilitating. The task in counselling is to accept and integrate these feelings, to explore and understand resistances to change, and to rechannel emotional energy into the new situation.

Part of the difficulty in adjusting to the new order of things is that it is so widespread that the outside world no longer offers the safety net it could once be relied upon to provide. It is not merely the structure of immediate reality that is changing: the structure of expectation has to change along with it, to keep pace with future developments in the wider job market. This is where personal and career development planning comes into the picture. Career counselling has always been a specialised area and this area in itself is now in a state of flux. The shift in employment practices from the job-for-life to short-term contract necessitates a whole new approach to the structuring of careers. The focus now is on building a portfolio of skills and experience to make an individual more marketable rather than on building a career in the linear sense that was standard practice for so many years. This trend makes life both inherently more unstable but also more exciting. It embraces both the shadow and the bright side of change. One large retail chain that established its own outplacement company found survivors were so envious of their former colleagues' opportunity to reappraise their lives that it responded with career development workshops for remaining staff. These have proved a huge success.

Referral
The communication phase of change programmes is quite clearly the province of management, and here skills training has proved in practice to be highly effective in helping to smooth this process.

For change-survivor counselling there is, in theory, no good reason why content-specific skills training should not enable in-house people – HR and line management – to do the job well. In practice, the sheer scale and time demand of such an operation might make it difficult to absorb into other functions, especially at such a stressful time. In such cases a professional specialist team on short-term contract would probably be a more viable proposition. Caution is also recommended where the unhappiness is so endemic as to make it impossible for those in-house people doing the counselling to take an independent view. If helpers are themselves vulnerable in a particular situation they will be of limited use to others, and might do actual harm.

Career counselling, on the other hand, is a purely specialist professional field. However, this has not stopped some organisations from creating highly successful career planning workshops. One large computer company runs a highly innovative programme (for trainees), that lays emphasis on autonomy and self-organised career development.*

Organisation change creates a space for individual introspection, both personal and professional. Skilled communication, counselling support, and career development planning provide the opportunity to confront the insecurities and turn them into challenges.

Post-trauma stress and critical incident debriefing

When we hear of post-trauma stress, words like Zeebrugge, Lockerbie and Hillsborough tend to spring to mind. Certainly, media coverage has heightened public awareness of the need to take special care of those affected by traumatic life events, but they have tended to concentrate on the dramatic and extraordinary. More 'ordinary' events such as bereavement and divorce can be equally traumatic to the individual, but only ever enter the headlines (if at all) as statistics.

Post-trauma stress is the name given to the development of certain symptoms or reactions following an abnormal and particularly distressing event. These events usually involve incidents such as rape, acts of violence, robberies, bombings,

*(Self-organised Learning is a concept developed by Professor Laurie Thomas and Dr Sheila Harri-Augstein of Brunel University's Centre for the Study of Human Learning.)

separation and divorce, war and combat, hostage-taking situations, disasters and accidents. 'Any major incident can have effects which are like the ripples on a pond when a stone is thrown into the water. They spread out in a widening circle of influence, affecting all they touch, until the energy is gradually dispersed,' writes Frank Parkinson.[6] The point he makes is that the immediate parties to a major event are not the only ones exposed to trauma: witnesses, rescue workers, relatives, helpers – all who are exposed to such an event – are candidates for the symptoms that have become associated with post-trauma stress. In this respect, survivor syndrome could also be classed as a form of post-trauma stress.

Symptoms, reactions and treatment
Parkinson defines post-trauma stress as 'the normal reactions of normal people to events which, for them, are unusual or abnormal'.[7] Even for those trained to do a difficult job, the effects can still be traumatic. Frequent exposure to horrific experiences might raise the threshold of tolerance. But doctors, police, rescue workers and the like can still be – and often are – traumatised by what they see and by what they sometimes have to do.

It is important to draw a distinction between post-trauma stress and *post-traumatic stress disorder* (PTSD). Post-trauma stress commonly affects those exposed to an incident but 'for different periods of time following the incident and in different intensity at the time or later. Some may be slightly distressed for a few hours or a few days and will then recover quite naturally and carry on with their lives. Others will suffer for longer and if the symptoms persist and intensify for more than a month they are usually identified as suffering from post-traumatic stress disorder and will need treatment.'[8] Psychological debriefing, or critical incident debriefing, as it is also known, should be on offer to all who are affected either directly or peripherally by a traumatic incident. The debriefing is a series of sessions on one day or over a few days, but is intended as one continuous process. PTSD needs longer-term help from a trained counsellor.

It is difficult to tell who is suffering. Going by visible signs is impossible. Though one person may be screaming and another might appear to be quite calm, this does not mean that the first is suffering from PTSD and the second is not. It also does not mean that the first is 'letting it all out' while the second is 'bottling it up'. Asking is not a reliable means of finding out, either, because denial is one of the most common reactions to a traumatic incident. I'm fine,' a sufferer will often say. This is one reason why professionally trained helpers are crucial.

The symptoms and reactions are wide-ranging and profound. They bear a marked resemblance to those of loss, even though the sufferer may not have experienced actual personal bereavement. Symptoms of both post-trauma stress and PTSD fall into three main categories:

☐ re-experiencing the feelings and emotions of the event, either as a result of some trigger sensation, or spontaneously. Flashbacks – vivid images of the event, nightmares and sleep-disturbances – these things can happen with frightening intensity, even many years later.

☐ avoidance – either by avoiding the subject or avoiding situations similar to those in which the event took place. Denial of the feelings is another form of avoidance, which inevitably leads to more prolonged and deeply rooted disturbance.

☐ arousal – heightened sensitivity to stimuli, such as noise; 'jumpiness'; erratic or volatile behaviour; mood swings; impulsiveness; obsession with vulnerability; or lapsing into depression and apathy; hyperactivity; aggressiveness and unreasonableness. Any of these symptoms will make the sufferer extremely difficult to live or work with.

The feelings aroused may include shame, anger, regret, blame, guilt, bitterness, isolation and loneliness, indecisiveness, and listlessness. Anxiety symptoms may include headaches, stomach pains, tightness in the head or chest, and many other non-specific pains which appear to have no physical cause; increased smoking or drinking; and increased or decreased sexual drive.

Managing post-trauma stress

Some working environments are particularly vulnerable to traumatic events and their employees live under constant threat, which is in itself a source of stress. Police and rescue services, the armed forces and medical and prison services are the public-sector workers most affected. The risks they face and the effects they suffer have become widely recognised. All of these professions are now served by teams of welfare specialists and, increasingly, by professional counsellors also. Private industry also has its high-risk areas, most notably in the financial sector. The consequence of stress for all of these employers is increased rates of absenteeism, poor employee health and problems in relationships, both domestic and professional.

The Post Office has taken an integrated approach to the problem. The Occupational Health Service identified the need for an effective trauma care programme in three of its businesses, the nature of whose work involved predictable levels of traumatic attack on employees. After careful analysis of the problem, their response was developed and then piloted for three years.

The approach comprised five distinct stages:

☐ Crisis management. A 'special relationship' was fostered with police authorities, who advised on developing clear procedures for handling hostage situations. Emergency contact procedures were set in place.

☐ Manager debrief.

☐ Psychological debriefing. This is a very specific procedure which we will refer to later. It can be carried out by trained professionals only. The debriefing session is normally followed up by a single session, at which time the debriefer decides whether or not to make a referral for trauma counselling. In instances where the trauma is less clearly defined, the debrief may be replaced by an individual stress assessment.

☐ Trauma counselling. This is carried out by qualified trauma counsellors on referral by the OHS doctor. In Cashco, it is available to family members who have been held hostage and in another business trauma counselling is available for family members if, in the view of the OHS doctor, the family member's trauma is having an adverse effect on the employee's well-being.

☐ Evaluation and follow-up. The progress of affected employees is carefully monitored. Post-incident questionnaires are used, and all employees who undertake a psychological debrief complete a satisfaction questionnaire.[9]

The pilot has been a resounding success, paying for itself in its first year. Sickness absence and medical retirement were reduced by half, and a breakdown of the cost of introducing the programme, measured against the savings accrued, revealed a bottom line saving of more than £100,000. The programme has now been introduced across the businesses.

Critical incident debriefing or psychological debriefing
This is a very specific technique developed by Dr Atle Dyregrov of the Centre for Crisis Psychology in Norway, following work done by the American, J.T. Mitchell. It is carried out by trained professional debriefers no sooner than 24 hours after the critical incident and preferably about 48 hours later. It should be done as soon as possible after that, because if it waits too long, feelings and emotions become too internalised. One or two debriefers conduct the session, which is done in groups seated around a table. Once the ground rules are explained and confidentiality is established, individual group members are helped to express their expectations, their impressions of and reactions to the incident, and guided into thinking about future coping strategies. The process is highly structured and disciplined, and designed to be as non-threatening as possible. Its purpose is to normalise reactions, reinforcing the fact that those suffering from post-trauma stress are not ill in any way, but experiencing normal symptoms of trauma and loss. Occasionally, but not always, there is a follow-up some time after the debriefing. This depends largely on the scale of the event.

It is worth noting, after a list of symptoms like the one above, that human beings are possessed of an extraordinary resilience. Even with support, those suffering extreme trauma do not ever forget it. In time the experience becomes incorporated with their inner world. But the support of friends and colleagues, coupled with professional debriefing and counselling support, offers the traumatised person the best possible chance of coping and recovering completely.

Stress is a normal and necessary part of life from birth right through to death, but excessive stress destroys health, relationships and even corporations. The challenge facing organisations is to devise strategies that deal with stress itself, and also to recognise and manage the causes.

References

1. COOPER C. and PAYNE R. (1994). *Causes, Coping and Consequences of Stress at Work*. Chichester, Wiley.
2. LAZARUS R. and FOLKMAN S. (1984). *Stress, Appraisal and Counselling*. New York, Springer.
3. FRIEDMAN M. and ULMER D. (1984). *Treating Type A Behaviour and Your Heart*. New York, Alfred A. Knopf Inc.
4. BROCKNER J., DEWITT R., GROVER S. and REED T. (1990). 'When it is especially important to explain why: factors affecting the relationship between managers' explanations of a layoff and survivors' reactions to the layoff.' *Journal of Experimental Social Psychology*. No. 26, pp. 389–407.
5. BROCKNER J., WIESENFELD B. M., REED T., GROVER S. and MARTIN C. (1993). 'Interactive effect of job content and context on the reactions of layoff survivors.' *Journal of Personality and Social Psychology*. No. 64, pp. 187–97.
6. PARKINSON F. (1993). *Post-trauma Stress*. London, Sheldon Press.
7. *Ibid.* p. 24.
8. *Ibid.* p. 25.
9. TEHRANI N. (1994). 'An integrated response to stress in three post office businesses'. Paper presented to the IPD conference in Harrogate, October 1994, and to be published in *Work and Stress* journal.

Further reading

DOHERTY N. and HORSTED J. (1995). 'Helping survivors to stay on board.' *People Management*, 12 January, pp. 26–9.

JACKSON P. R. (1993). 'The reactions of those who survive lay-offs: a digest of recent research.' *International Journal of Selection and Assessment*, Vol. 1, No. 4, October, p. 244–6.
ROSS R. R. and ALTMAIER E. M. (1994). *Intervention in Occupational Stress*. London, Sage.

7

OUTPLACEMENT COUNSELLING

It was a grey Monday morning one November when the 60 or so employees of a well-known city bank arrived at the plush reception area. There followed a scene that many who work as outplacement consultants will be familiar with. The employees were handed a cardboard box containing their personal belongings and told to report to the human resources department, and that an outplacement counsellor would be available to see them after they had been given the bad news. This is a brutal scene; however, in cases where high security is needed and sabotage is entirely possible it may have been a necessary precaution.

Organisational starting-points

Whatever our views may be of this particular example, it may leave us wondering why this type of treatment is duplicated in situations that do not have such special security needs. It is an unfortunate fact that not all organisations finding that they have to embark on the sad duty of downsizing seek out good practice. Those that do, tend to consider different ways of handling the situation – for example, by not telling people the bad news just as they are about to go on holiday, or last thing on a Friday, and by training those unlucky enough to be in the position of having to tell people that they have lost their jobs in how to go about things. This is often called 'breaking the news' training. This kind of training contains a mix of communication and counselling skills, eg listening, observing, open questions and reflecting back.

The training helps the manager to give the message in a clear and humane way whilst being aware of, and picking up, signals that a person may need immediate counselling support. There is also the consideration that the managers themselves will need some support: it is a difficult job to do and emotionally draining.

People react to the news in different ways. Some are glad and some relieved. The majority, however, will display a range of emotions from shock to anger, depression, and a massive drop in self-esteem. This is why organisations who want to get it right either call in outplacement consultants to pick these people up immediately and counsel them, or, alternatively, train their HR and other suitable managers in the type of counselling skills needed to handle such events.

Despite the existence of those organisations which make an attempt to get things right, there undoubtedly exist those that do not. The horror stories are numerous.

Surveying a number of consultants who have worked in outplacement, the consensus is that this kind of scenario and the ensuing reactions are still common. People who suffer the loss of a job react in a very similar way to those who have experienced a bereavement. As outlined in Chapter 5, bereavement is a process, not a state, with people eventually coming out of the other end of the tunnel. The way that people are told and subsequently treated in outplacement situations seems to have a direct relationship with their emergence into 'daylight'.

Typical reactions

There is often a clear emotional pattern that people experience, called the transition curve (see Figure 7). A common reaction on hearing the bad news is lack of acceptance. This can be clearly seen in people for whom there is a long time-lag between being told the news and actually leaving. Characteristically, they stay in a fantasy phase and, after the initial reaction, convince themselves that the organisation has made a mistake and will change its mind. This manifests itself in their tendency to put more effort than they have ever done into their jobs. It is only as time wears on and leaving becomes a reality that they drop down the curve into capitulation and become depressed. It is at this point that counselling becomes essential. Outplacement counsellors have the most rewarding part of the process: taking people at their lowest ebb and building them up in confidence and strength so that they can find a new job.

Figure 7
THE TRANSITION CURVE AND JOB LOSS

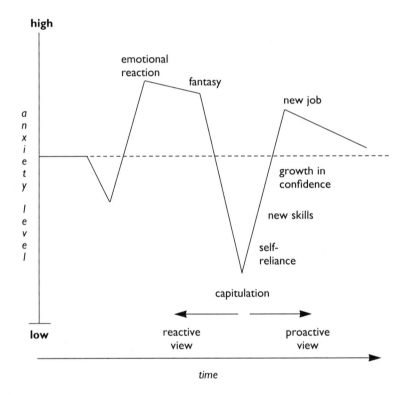

After Hopson & Adams, 1976[1]

Setting aside the humanitarian implications of all of this and taking a purely pragmatic approach, neglecting these issues of good practice can only be bad news in terms of the long-term public relations of the organisation. It is often said that when one person receives bad customer service, or has a bad experience with an organisation, they tell seven other people . . . who tell seven others, and so on. A good way to lose customers.

Good practice in outplacement

In a highly memorable conversation a few years ago, the then managing director of a rather well-known outplacement agency remarked, 'Outplacement is about coaching and job search, senior executives don't have emotional problems.' Many senior managers will doubtless be pleased to hear this. Outplacement counselling has existed as a service for over 20 years in the UK and for somewhat longer in the USA. It is only relatively recently, however, that it has been seen as a process that involves both counselling and coaching, and not just coaching. Even so, there are some who still do not see the counselling content in the process.

Those working as outplacement counsellors often report that the way that people are told has a great impact on how long they take to recover from the situation. People remember how they were treated for some time after they have recovered from the hurt of being made redundant. This hurt or anger will often continue even when they are long into enjoying their new jobs.

Take the case of 'X', who was a top-level manager within a large multinational pharmaceutical company. In conversation with him, two years later, he still recounts with bitterness the way he was told that he was leaving and all but frog-marched out of the building. This was after almost 20 years of outstandingly good performance and loyalty. So much for respect, empathy and genuineness (see Chapters 4 and 8 for more on these words). His ongoing feelings are not about losing the job (he had recognised that the company culture had changed and was becoming incompatible with his personal values) but the fact that he was treated like yesterday's news. It should be said that he now occupies a top-level post with a prestigious company, and is very successful.

The issue here is how and when the bad news is given and how people are handled inbetween that event and the time that they leave or are given outplacement support.

Much has been achieved through the publishing of a Code of Conduct by the Institute of Personnel and Development, and by the forming of special groups where those involved in outplacement and career counselling can discuss professional

issues. Some organisations select internal outplacement consultants and provide them with training. Some have internally run job shops and counselling support centres. For
human resource professionals and senior managers working
in organisations that do not have a need for such ongoing
internal support, the issue is about choosing a good external
supplier. For these people, reading the Code of Conduct is a
must (see Further Reading). But more is needed.

Who to turn to

Outplacement consultancies have been accused of shrouding
the process in mystery. HR managers have told the authors
that it is hard to find out exactly what goes on behind the
'oak-panelled doors'. Whilst there is undoubtedly much
expertise in the process, we believe that buyers of the service
should be able to make informed decisions. Having said this,
it is not an easy matter to become informed as to exactly what
constitutes a quality service. We have created the following
check-list to help organisations select a good supplier. Whilst
the list is not definitive it should provide some useful starting
points.

Quality check-list

Outplacement support centres/job shops

Centre manager
- ☐ Has previous experience including a track record of successful placements.
- ☐ Is a strong marketer. For example, actively publicises the
  centre and its client to local and national organisations.
  Personally visits local employers.
- ☐ Is trained in the coaching and counselling skills needed
  and can coach their team.
- ☐ Has acquired counselling training and experience from a
  reputable organisation and in enough depth to ensure
  understanding of the essential ethical issues, the referrral
  process, specific personal issues that commonly arise, use

of the skills and supervision. Are they an active member of the British Association for Counselling?

☐ Either personally, or externally, sets up proper counselling supervision for the team.

☐ Has in-depth knowledge of the mechanics of the outplacement process, including all stages of self-analysis, self-marketing and job search strategy (see later in this chapter for more detailed definitions).

☐ Can administer or arrange for psychometric profiling of clients.

☐ Has the right personal qualities, eg is mature, personable and can cope well with pressure.

Individual outplacement consultants

☐ These have a background that enables them to realistically coach their clients. For example, have organisational and, preferably, management experience including recruitment and the selection process, effective presentation (written and speech craft), influencing skills, impression management and assertiveness.

☐ They have the right counselling experience and training, (as for the centre manager).

☐ They are good problem-solvers who, for example, can discover the reasons why an individual's job-search campaign is not working, and put it right.

Outplacement agencies

☐ The facilities that an agency provides will dramatically affect both the individual and support centre programmes. These should include on-line data bases such as Textline, company listings and local directories. A good reference library service and the provision of newspapers and journals are both essential.

☐ Good administration support will make all the difference to the speed and efficiency with which CVs are typed and letters dispatched. There should be adequate secretarial support, a good word-processing system with a mail-merge facility and, ideally, desk-top publishing.

☐ Networking should be a normal part of the service. Agencies should be willing to share their own business contacts for the benefit of their clients.

☐ Expert advice provided on such things as small business start-up, self-employment and pensions/financial issues.

It almost goes without saying, but if an outplacement company offers added value, over and above these basic items, they may be hungrier for your business and likely to make a better job of it. Essential for selecting setting up an internal service, and useful in selecting external suppliers, will be your understanding of the items on the checklist. It will put you one step ahead. The next section will also help.

The outplacement process: a blend of coaching and counselling

The skill in outplacement counselling is the ability to switch constantly between coaching and counselling according to the messages that a client (counsellee) is giving out. Coaching is the imparting of information and counselling is drawing it out. The consultant may start with a counselling approach, eg allowing the client to ventilate their feelings about the situation. Unenlightened counsellors may assume that they have dealt with the emotional issues simply by allowing such ventilation. However, the following illustrates how counselling and coaching feed off each other throughout the process.

The outplacement process contains several stages through which the counsellor takes the person in order to help them find a new job, become self-employed, set up their own business, or retire. The stages can include:

☐ initial scene setting and skills and strengths analysis
☐ reality testing (constraints and development needs)
☐ options planning
☐ CV writing
☐ interview practice
☐ job search strategies
☐ time management.

It may surprise some readers to discover that each stage contains both coaching and counselling issues.

Initial scene setting/skills and strengths analysis. The first session will inevitably involve exploration of the situation that led to the outplacement and the person's current thoughts and feelings about the decision. Most people, even when they see a sound business reason why the organisation needs to cut back, feel 'junked', ie that they have been placed on the scrap heap. Some people are pleased, eg if they are near retirement and will be leaving with a financial package and an enhanced pension. But this is relatively rare. It is wise to follow this initial discussion, however long it takes, with the start of the skills and strengths analysis phase, as this immediately starts to heal bruised self-esteem.

Using a number of exercises as starting-points, the process involves drawing out information that the person is unlikely to see for themselves, such as, how often do we stop to analyse the skills that we are employing in our day-to-day work? This analysis can involve the use of psychometric testing, or personality profiling.

Coaching There is low content at this stage, although an informative 'intervention' may be useful in the beginning to explain typical reactions to job loss, or how long on average they can expect to be job searching before finding a new position. Counsellors often use the transition curve (see Figure 7). For example, informing someone that they may go through a fantasy stage where they may not believe that they are actually leaving can be useful to help the person recognise what is happening to them.

Counselling As mentioned earlier, people generally react emotionally to being made redundant. These emotions can include any or several of the following: anger, hurt, loss of confidence, shock, depression, panic, resignation, disbelief–belief. People can also be optimistic and relieved (most people would rather know than be left in a state of uncertainty). They could also, of course, be happy to go.

Counselling skills are needed to draw out information, and to allow people some time and space to express their feelings. 'Reflecting' may be needed to help the person to release emotion and to discover their own skills and strengths. Most people do not think about such things when they are happily employed and then, temporarily, lose belief in them when made redundant. The process of creating a list of such skills and strengths is therapeutic in that it builds back the person's lost confidence (see Chapter 4 for more on counselling skills). Some counsellors list the skills and strengths on a flipchart and post them on the wall. This helps the person to see their 'assets' building up throughout the sessions and adds a potency to the healing process.

A counselling contract of confidentiality will need to be set up for trust to develop. The counsellor will need to make a statement to the effect that confidentiality will be kept; this also presupposes that the counsellor has received training that encompasses ethical considerations.

It may well be that any current personal problems that the person has will emerge at this early stage, eg marital or relationship difficulties. However, some clients need a warm-up period before they will disclose such information, so it is important for counsellors to be aware that this can happen at any time during the process.

Reality testing/options planning

Here the counsellor may feed back the results of personality profiles or ask for some notes from a person who knows the client well. These are just two of many exercises that can be used here.

Coaching If a development need is recognised in the form of a skill gap or a career problem then coaching can be useful. Examples of such needs could be poor interpersonal skills, unassertive style, lack of influencing ability, selling skills, teambuilding, bad organising skills and a range of what could be called technical abilities. If the skills and strengths analysis has been thorough then the options planning stage becomes easier. New career opportunities may emerge as transferable skills are discovered ie those skills that will be useful in a different job role. Equally, a cherished fantasy about a particular job role may not stand the test of reality.

Counselling Clearly, it can be hard for people to come up against their limitations, or the fact that they have been in a job that does not play to their strengths. Sensitive challenging, or confronting, may be needed to help them see this and to help them to change direction if the issues are too fundamental to their character and style to be addressed through coaching. Of course, the confronting can be with good news as well as bad as transferable skills unfold. Some people may have just as much difficulty accepting their strengths as they do their weaknesses. This is especially true if the person has been in a bullying type of culture, or has had an oppressive boss who demeaned them.

CV writing

There are as many opinions about what is a good CV as there are actual CVs. Many who write them would agree on certain characteristics, such as the length and layout. However, because of the diversity of opinion the views below must remain idiosyncratic, based on the authors' own experience of what works well.

Coaching Most people take a very conventional approach to their CV, believing that it should be a factual account of their career history. A coaching intervention that often needs to be made is that, whilst it should be factual, it should also be seen as a marketing document – if you like, an advertisement that will excite the 'buyer' into action. The action is that of granting the person an interview. The ease with which the CV is written will depend on how well the skills and strengths analysis part of the programme has been carried out. This part of the programme provides the material for the CV as skills, strengths, achievements and personal attributes are explored. Bearing this in mind, beware the organisation, or individual, who offers a 'quick fix' CV without this necessary preparation. Another point to consider is that the person being counselled may not be good with words, and some writing ability will be needed on the part of the counsellor. Most experienced outplacement counsellors would agree on the following basic guidelines:

☐ A short summary, sometimes called a '30-second advertisement', should appear somewhere on the front page.

This should tell the reader in a succinct way what the person has achieved and what they have to offer.

☐ The front page should not be crowded, but have a few (about six) two- or three-line sentences about the major areas of experience or achievements. The maximum white space around the information will make it easy for the reader to pick out the important points. Personal details and education should appear; however, these facts should not take up half the page of valuable space needed for more enticing information. The suggestion is that these details are summarised at the bottom of the page.

☐ The following pages (not more than two) should then give details of the organisations worked for, responsibilities and specific job-related achievements.

Counselling The lack of confidence that is common with people who have been made redundant can interfere just as easily at the CV stage as at any earlier time. They may not fully 'buy into' their own skills and strengths and this can interfere with the information that they present during the interview stage (more on this shortly). Gentle confronting is needed to remind the person of their skills and strengths (see Chapter 4 for more on confronting). Often they have a blind spot about these, seeing only that the organisation did not wish to retain them. Once again, informative interventions can be useful, eg exploring the reasons for the redundancy programme in a way that shows that many factors are taken into consideration, the least of which is the person's actual performance and ability. Often the reasons are to do with politics, as revealed by a well-known piece of research called the 'N Factor'.

An important point to realise is that the client will not always take in such information at the first meeting and it may need to be brought out several times during the programme. People are often in a state of shock and will take some time to recover and, as we know, people who are in shock won't hear all that is being said to them.

Interview practice It is probably clear at this stage that the balance will generally shift from counselling to coaching as you move through the programme. By the time that the interview stage is reached, most of the drawing out of information will have taken place and the person will need to be given some techniques for the interview. The art of answering questions is different from that of asking them, and whilst much has been written and many training courses exist for recruiters, interviewees will not so readily find such guidelines.

Coaching Outplacement consultants need to have some in-depth knowledge of good communication technique. They will also need to know which typical interview questions are likely to arise. Most outplacement firms have printed manuals containing such information. Once again, the stages that have gone before come into play. For example a good CV not only gets an interview for the person, but also provides a 'hook' to elicit the right questions from the interviewer so that answers can be rehearsed. It should also be said that rehearsal is the vital component. Aside from this, the counsellor should cover use of language (creating what are sometimes called 'word pictures') to make the answers memorable, eg use of speech craft, such as voice modulation and pausing and pacing. Non-verbal communication should be covered, which will include using positive, open body language, wearing the right clothes and 'impression management', ie creating the right impression within the first 30 seconds of the interview to manage the famous 'halo effect' that all trained recruiters will be familiar with.

The most effective form for feedback to the interviewee is the use of audiotape and video recordings to play back the person's performance and to give them some insight into their style. Here a counselling approach can be vital to gain acceptance of the need to change.

Counselling Interpersonal Process Recall, or IPR, provides a powerful way of giving feedback, especially where the person lacks confidence in putting their answers across. (See Chapter 10 for more on IPR.) Sitting alongside the client and viewing the video play-back, the counsellor can explore any points that are not coming over in the right way. For example, the counsellor might ask, 'When you talked about that achievement you did not sound very confident – what was going through your mind at the time?' It almost goes without saying, but all video feedback needs to be handled with sensitivity, especially if the person has not seen themselves on video before. The counsellor should position the session by explaining that video is not the most flattering of media and that most people are not generally pleased with how they appear.

Job search strategies/time management

This stage in the process will be of particular help to those clients who have stayed with one organisation for a number of years. In any case, people may not have up-to-date knowledge of the job market at any particular time. Most people will certainly not be aware of the different methods of job searching, aside from the more obvious replying to advertisements. Strategies will include approaches to recruitment consultants and executive search specialists; contact development (popularly known as networking); and direct approaches to selected organisations.

Coaching The counsellor will need specialist knowledge of the various strategies, which will often boil down to good communication and influencing skills. For example, the approach of seeking advice from a networking contact rather than asking them for a job will make the encounter, at the least, less embarrassing for both and, at the most, flattering for the contact.

Knowledge of the market-place is more readily available than most people would suppose. Surveys exist on which types of job are on the increase and which are on the way out. This can provide valuable information to aid decisions about retraining or how to position existing transferable skills. A current example is that contract work is on the increase. This will be good news for those in the older age groups seeking to fill a few years with some work before retirement.

Most professional outplacement firms will provide written manuals containing job search strategies and suggestions for time management. It is then left to the counsellor to set appropriate targets for each individual.

Counselling It is not so much at this stage, but in the review meetings that follow, that counselling needs can emerge. In fact, it is often at this stage that people feel in need of the most support. Apart from the more obvious issue of having to deal with rejection letters, there may be situations where people do not carry out their agreed targets. This can happen because they suddenly experience a reactive depression at the reality of being out in the job market. They have had a period of time feeling supported and even cosseted by their counsellor and now they are on their own.

There have even been cases of people being inactive in their search because they do not want to work again, or, as with one person who realised that he never wanted to be a manager in the first place and wanted a change, but did not know how to handle the social pressure that this decision would bring. Experienced counsellors will know that no behaviour happens in a vacuum, ie without a cause. Less experienced people will need to get into the habit of being aware of such possibilities and use the skills needed to draw out such information, by active listening, questioning and reflecting.

Why counselling is undervalued

As can be seen from this overview of the coaching and counselling aspects of outplacement, those who deny the counselling aspects may not be speaking from a position of experience. The coaching/counselling mix will be different with each individual; some may need more of one and less of the other according to their own situation and well-being. The judgement about which interventions to use must be taken on a personal basis. However, it has been known for some outplacement consultants, who do not feel comfortable with counselling, to collude with their clients not to cover painful emotional issues.

A criticism that we have heard is that 'counsellors will look for what is not there', ie will invent counselling issues that do not exist, simply because they can handle them. If the outplacement process is properly understood, consultants properly trained, and individuals handled on an individual basis, it is hard to see how this can happen.

From the authors' point of view, experience has taught that it is possible to be surprised by counselling needs when you least expect them, ie when you have judged that the person needs mainly coaching rather than counselling and that they are basically coping well. To illustrate, and to end this chapter, here is a true story.

An outplacement counsellor received a telephone call from a client who had been in his new job for about five months. He had previously worked with a large electronics company for a number of years and had been a committed 'company man'. On the morning that the counsellor received the call the client had woken up feeling unexpectedly depressed. He had gone through his outplacement programme with vigour, thinking to himself that he would 'show them how they had made a mistake, by getting a good new job as soon as possible'. He achieved his goal, and anger against the organisation was the spur. But on this particular morning he felt depressed, so he rang his outplacement counsellor. After some exploration it became clear that he had realised that he was no longer an 'X' (the previous employer) company man. He would never again feel part of an organisation that had been his life for about 10 years. This was despite the fact that he was in an excellent new job. His anger had served the purpose of providing impetus, which had not been a bad thing at the time, but he had simply not allowed himself time to grieve over his last job. He needed to do this before he could emerge from the tunnel for good. Bereavement feelings in outplacement cut deep.

References

1. HOPSON B. and ADAMS J. (1976). 'Towards an understanding of transition.' In J. Adams, J. Hayes, and B. Hopson (eds) *Transition: understanding and managing personal change*. Martin Robertson.

Further reading

EGGERT M. (1991). *Outplacement: A guide to management and delivery*. London, Institute of Personnel Management.

INSTITUTE OF PERSONNEL AND DEVELOPMENT (1994). *The IPD Code of Conduct for Career and Outplacement Consultants.* London, IPD.

MILNE T. (1989). 'Counselling in the context of redundancy and unemployment.' In W. Dryden, D. Charles-Edwards and R. Woolfe (eds) *Handbook of Counselling in Britain.* London, Tavistock Press.

PART 3

TRAINING GUIDELINES

8

COUNSELLING, COACHING AND MENTORING

There seems little doubt that organisations in the 1990s are demonstrating a consistent trend in the way that they are structured. This trend is towards much 'flatter' hierarchies than have been seen in the past. In practical terms this means that senior managers have more contact with, and direct responsibility for, larger numbers of people on a day-to-day basis.

With the buffer removed between that manager and his/her group, their ability to manage the people, as well as the business aspects of their job, becomes vital. It is also likely that they will need to delegate to others some of the tasks that have been traditionally their remit; hence the move towards self-managing teams that has become popular in a number of organisations.

Many organisations have become leaner and this has meant that they have had to deal with the process of outplacement. Aside from this, organisations need to be aware that how they manage the downsizing process will have a great impact on the way that the leavers will react, and on how the 'survivors' will feel about continuing to give their commitment to the organisation. The 'survivor syndrome' results in lowered commitment and stress-type reactions when it is not properly managed.

Some would argue that never before has a manager's ability to take on the role of coach, and sometimes counsellor, become more necessary. It is also timely to review the usefulness of the idea of managers being mentors to their people. Much has been written on the subject of mentoring and, in keeping with the context of this book, we will look specifically at how counselling skills and approaches can aid the mentoring relationship.

A toolkit for managers

Clearly, organisations can only benefit at this time from the awareness that managers need to become stronger in the skills of performance management. They will need to acquire the communication skills of counselling described in Chapter 4 of this book. However, if they are to engage people's commitment, more is needed. They will need to adopt a counselling approach that displays respect, empathy and genuineness. But what exactly do we mean by respect, empathy and genuineness in the context of performance management? What are the behaviours that bring the words to life? In terms of management behaviour, they could be defined as:

Respect

☐ gives time and attention to people (two very precious resources in today's world of work)

☐ takes others seriously

☐ takes notice of what other people say

☐ is courteous

☐ does not jump to conclusions

☐ avoids put-downs or sarcasm

☐ is not controlling

☐ keeps commitments

☐ keeps confidentiality

☐ allows other people to take decisions and to make mistakes

☐ assumes other people are worth knowing

☐ values people equally.

Empathy

☐ is interested in others' well-being

☐ sees others' point of view, ie can put themselves in another's shoes

☐ imagines what other people must be feeling

☐ listens and reflects back others' thoughts and feelings

☐ does not attribute motives to others, or assume knowledge of what they are thinking and feeling

☐ openly explores others' points of view, without prejudice.

Genuineness

- □ does not pretend
- □ is consistent – does what they say they will do
- □ does not have a 'facade'
- □ is sincere
- □ is honest and open
- □ is prepared to apologise or admit ignorance
- □ sticks to what they have agreed
- □ keeps promises.

A further and most important point is that there is also a trend towards devolving what have traditionally been human resource activities to line managers. Today's HR managers will need to help their management teams to acquire such skills and, whether the trend continues or not, this can only enrich the manager's ability to develop and lead their people. They will need to consider:

Coaching The counselling/coaching mix in performance management.

Mentoring What is meant by effective mentoring relationships. It will also be useful to consider:

Psychometric profiling Personality profiles and management style inventories. Their use is widespread and if used well they can aid the performance management process.

The role of the human resources manager

Human resource professionals are in a good position to deliver coaching and mentoring support in the context of performance management. In management terms they can function independently from the line, providing an objective view. An excellent application of counselling skills can be seen when an HR manager mentors a senior person on how to develop their staff using a combination of counselling and coaching techniques. Unlike the external counsellor, they know the organisation because they are part of it. They can advise individuals on how to traverse the slopes of the organisational culture and politics, as well as helping them to handle relationships and know their own skills and strengths. They can help people to test reality against their career aspirations.

At this point it may be useful to remind ourselves of the difference between coaching and counselling. In simple terms, coaching involves the imparting of information and counselling, drawing it out. In both coaching and counselling the establishing of a good interpersonal relationship is important, and some of the skills are similar, eg active listening, using open questions and summarising.

Much has been written about coaching methods and the different styles that people can adopt. As this book is more concerned with counselling at work, these two aspects of coaching will not be examined.

The coaching/counselling mix

In terms of the performance management process as a whole, there are points at which coaching and counselling clearly interweave when someone has a career problem. In performance management, as with any other communication context, personal problems come into play. These problems are many and varied and some common situations have been discussed in Chapter 5. In the specific context of career issues, friction can be caused by problems to do with working relationships, eg not being able to work well with other members of a team or not getting on well with the boss. The giving and receiving of feedback is a sensitive issue. Mostly managers give feedback and, where a healthy relationship exists, they also receive it. More on this later.

Giving feedback on performance

How many of us have inadvertently glanced into a mirror and noticed that our hair was untidy or, horror of horrors, we had a smudge of dirt on our nose? Of course, it would have been impossible to know either of these things had we not looked in the mirror. Giving feedback can be seen as 'holding up the mirror' to enable people to see how they are doing in their jobs. It could be argued that without such feedback no change can take place. Change, in this context, is about reinforcing what is going well and helping the person to improve what is not. Some starting points for giving feedback are given in this checklist of basic dos and don'ts.

Do
☐ check your motivation for giving someone feedback
☐ give feedback as immediately as possible
☐ respect people's need for a private discussion
☐ be honest and 'up front'
☐ recognise the positive aspects to people's performance as well as the negatives
☐ focus on specific performance examples, relating to things which actually happen in people's jobs
☐ make your discussion two-way; ask questions, check reactions, etc.
☐ vary your style according to the needs of the individual and the situation
☐ focus on helping to move someone's performance forward
☐ be tentative about information that is not completely clear.

Don't
☐ use feedback as an opportunity to 'have a go' at someone
☐ leave it until days or weeks later
☐ avoid it entirely during career discussion
☐ discuss people's performance in public
☐ avoid discussing difficult issues, like poor performance
☐ dwell on the negatives and get caught up in destructive criticism
☐ make personal remarks
☐ conduct monologues with people or pay lip service to their agreement
☐ be inflexible, ie not responding to people's reactions
☐ dwell on the past without thinking and talking about the future.

As mentioned earlier, feedback can be a form of giving praise, by reflecting and expanding on what is going well and giving criticism by confronting what is not going well. Reflecting and confronting are both counselling skills. In both of these situations a counselling approach can make all the difference to how the person receives the message. Adopting an attitude of respect, empathy and genuineness will mean that an adult-to-adult conversation takes place. Such conversations can be described as 'assertive transactions' where the person receiving the feedback feels that they are valued and respected. This is a very basic point that is often overlooked in more controlling cultures.

As we are generally rather poor at giving praise (natural British reserve?) focusing on the behaviour can be a help. The same will apply to giving criticism. The temptation is to become aggressive or too personal, where a focus on the facts will enable the person to see what they need to do differently. It is the difference between saying 'I thought that your report was lousy' and saying 'the report that you wrote was clearly laid out and well written. Some of the points needed more detail, for example . . .' With the latter message the person knows what they need to do differently next time, and does not take the criticism as a personal affront. The right conditions for coaching are created so that the person receiving the feedback is not made to feel that asking for help is an admission of failure.

Some managers may have difficulty with this in their own career development. Often the expectation from them is they are 'meant to know'. The higher up you are in an organisation, the more this applies. There is an obvious counselling need here and this may explain the growth of such services as 'executive coaching' where an external consultant will seem a safer person for managers to open up to. (There is also much prestige associated with bringing in an expensive consultant.) The sign of a good coach is the ability to move effortlessly between coaching and counselling as required.

A partnership approach

An exciting development in performance management is the moves that some organisations are making towards initiating career counselling where no problem has presented itself.

Some promote a partnership approach, with the organisation and its employees taking equal responsibility for career development. One such example is found in one organisation that has brought in career guidance workshops for all levels of managers as part of a performance management programme. They are doing this to provide greater knowlege of what individuals have to offer in a broader context than their current job role; the creation of a kind of 'skills bank' founded on the notion that skills are transferrable between jobs. This is truly innovative as people in organisations are often seen as capable of their current job only.

Many people report that it is only when they are outplaced that they are introduced to the idea of transferable skills and experience career counselling for the first time. Career counsellors working in organisations will tell you that the processes that they employ are not dissimilar to the outplacement processes described in Chapter 7. They adapt to the individual needs, but often use a process that includes the same elements of skills, strengths and attributes analysis, psychometric profiling, reality testing and options planning. However, the difference is significant.

Understanding the context
Career counsellors working within organisations who have not had workplace experience may find themselves on a steep learning curve.

We have made the point before that some professional counsellors may have difficulty getting into the organisational world. This can result in the counsellor losing out on the opportunity to translate counselling into a new field of work and the organisation missing the opportunity to see the benefits that can result from counselling. Clearly, HR managers need to check out the level of organisational understanding when contracting counsellors into the organisation.

Personal and relationship problems in career counselling
It would be making a false distinction to separate career issues from the picture of the person's life as a whole. For

example, the desire for a more interesting job may be a reflection of a life stage, or be linked to issues outside of work – say, an underdeveloped social life. Also, a long-standing problem which has been tolerated may have become intolerable by a 'last straw' event, eg working late hours and then suddenly being asked to work a weekend. It is also often the case that career success is partly linked with social or interpersonal skills, eg the person is good at their job but perceived in some way as aggressive or 'difficult'. As the case-studies in this chapter illustrate, we have experienced many-faceted problems linked with career issues. These have included: lack of self-confidence/self-esteem; desire for autonomy and independence (in a controlling culture); low tolerance for change and the inability to cope with personal stress.

In such situations it seems obvious that a high degree of counselling skill needs to be exercised before coaching can take place. Trained counsellors will also need a wide repertoire of management skills and information that they can impart at the coaching stage of the relationship. Developing an assertive style, coaching others, presentation and influencing skills are some of the things that may be called for along with more technical management skills.

A point that we have made before is that, in this context, it is clear that the 'pure counselling' approach offered by a personal therapist will be of limited use.

Three cases

The counselling/coaching mix is clearly present in the three cases described here. What is significant is how this mix was applied in each situation. In career counselling, individuals need an individual approach, and each case should be viewed as different from the last.

'Bob' is a sales executive working for a high tech organisation. His largest account has a multimillion pound potential and, up until the time that things started to go wrong, he has managed it well. Bob's manager first became concerned about him when he noticed how much Bob was drinking. He would take two-hour lunches in the pub and then be moody in the afternoons. Combined with this, his sales performance had dropped and he was making fewer appointments for demonstrations than ever before. Cold-calling for new customers was practically non-existent. Not wanting to lose someone who had been a consistent high performer for six years, the manager called in an external counsellor. (The company had a very small HR team and they did not feel that they had the skills to cope with the situation.)

Two issues emerged. Bob had a long-standing alcohol problem that tended to worsen at times of difficulty. The other issue was that the style of selling in the organisation had changed from one of demonstration and the 'technical sell' to one of building client relationships. This was because the people involved in his account wanted to do business in a different way. Having uncovered the first issue the counsellor referred Bob to a specialist alcohol counsellor, and dealt with the second issue herself. Bob was coached in how to give persuasive presentations, and in the techniques of selling using a blend of input of information followed by role play using CCTV. He felt his confidence increase along with his skills, and embarked on a strategy to stop drinking (supported by the specialist counsellor) and to set himself new performance objectives. He is still doing well.

'Richard' was a financial director who tended to lose his motivation and commitment after a period of time in the job. His managing director was concerned that he was suddenly coming in late and leaving early and that he was generally more downbeat in his attitude. As a routine procedure, Richard was asked to write a biographical summary of his early years (before he started work) along with some other exercises focusing on skills and strengths.

What emerged was that Richard had had a very unusual childhood. He had been placed in a boarding school at the tender age of four years whilst his father occupied a diplomatic post abroad. He grew up without a father figure to relate to, and subsequently became a poor father to his own children. In the context of his career, he tended to choose bosses whom he could almost hero-worship. Naturally, he was constantly being disappointed when his heroes turned out to have feet of clay. At this point he would lose motivation and seek another job. The key to breaking this pattern was the clarification of the problem uncovered by counselling. Richard also needed some coaching on how to behave in a more assertive way, he tended to be unassertive in style and this did not always work for him in gaining the respect of his boss and colleagues. Richard's attitude to his boss is a good illustration of the phenomenon of 'transference' outlined briefly in Chapter 4, under psychodynamic theory.

'Sheila' had been a marketing director in an electronics company for three years. She had always had bosses who admired her somewhat aggressive and forthright style; she was known not to suffer fools gladly. When a chief executive came along who had a more understated style and who felt less secure about himself, Sheila's behaviour was seen as threatening by him. She would openly argue with him in front of others, which he found acutely embarrassing. The human resources manager, seeing the dangers of the situation, suggested that Sheila talk over her style and relationship with her boss with an independent counsellor. The HR manager in this case has to be admired for the counselling skill needed to get Sheila to see that she had a problem and agree to get help. The counsellor helped Sheila to talk through her relationship with her boss. Using a mix of gentle confronting and dyadic questioning, Sheila was helped to see things from the boss's point of view. She was then ready to try out some different behaviours. It took some time for the relationship to improve and Sheila needed continued support to reinforce the new behaviours. If Sheila had been sacked, the organisation would have lost a talented person and she, almost certainly, would have repeated the same pattern of behaviour in her next job, and failed again.

A point for consideration is that we cannot assume that all career problems have a personal cause; neither can we assume that they have not. Coaching without counselling would not give us the information to make the right decision about the cause, and counselling without coaching would not have the right effect.

The managers of the people described in the case studies were open enough to admit the idea that performance problems can have a personal cause. A manager moving too soon into disciplinary mode can be problematic for the organisation, not only in terms of the possibility of losing talent, but in risking an unfair dismissal case. This consideration reinforces the need for counselling skills training for managers in the context of performance management. Such training becomes even more important when we think of mentoring, a process that relies heavily on a long-term one-to-one relationship between managers and their reports.

Mentoring

Mentor 1: *cap:* a friend of Odysseus entrusted with the education of Odysseus' son, Telemachus **2**: a trusted counsellor or guide **3**: TUTOR, COACH.

(Webster)

Nowadays, mentoring is seen as a process whereby mentor and mentoree work together to discover and develop the mentoree's potential. The goal is not promotion; rather it is enabling the 'mentoree' to develop his or her abilities. We have already referred to the fact that many organisations have flatter management structures and this may account for an increased interest in mentoring as a possible development tool. A good manager can nurture ability in his or her team so as to delegate duties and allow the growth of self-managing teams. However, there are some issues that will need to be addressed before mentoring can work well.

Managers may lack the ability to recognise a potential high-flyer or, if they do, be reluctant to lose that employee by encouraging them to move to another area of the company. 'Managers who are unavailable, uncommitted, or who dislike particular subordinates can effectively block the career paths of talented employees and prevent them from realising their potential.'[1] They may also lack the time, especially in organisations where over-enthusiastic slimming down means that they expect one manager to do the job of two. The latest Industrial Society survey on mentoring describes how it has taken over from coaching as the most popular form of management training by about 40 per cent of organisations, but it also makes the point that managers often lack the time to do it. (See Further Reading.)

The setting up of a mentoring programme is a significant

policy issue for organisations and the pros and cons need to be considered carefully. One point that seems clear in all that has been written on mentoring is this: mentors breed mentors. The future talent of an organisation could depend on such a process. Certainly, those who can identify someone in their past who mentored them, describe the experience as having a profound effect on their careers.

What makes a good mentor?

Clearly, becoming a mentor requires a special type of commitment from a manager. To quote Carl Rogers, 'the degree to which I can create relationships that will facilitate the growth of others, as separate persons, is the measure of growth I have achieved in myself . . .'[2] Carl Rogers was, of course, speaking from a counselling focus, which brings us back to this issue: adopting an attitude of respect, empathy and genuineness, with all of the practical behaviours suggested earlier in this chapter, will provide the conditions for such a relationship to occur.

Taking Rogers' words one step further, another dimension to consider is that managers themselves will benefit from becoming mentors. Some of the more specific benefits might be alternative ways of behaving towards employees that will build on what is working, and improve what is not working, in their styles. They may more easily receive as well as give feedback. Developing such people's handling abilities will be especially useful for managers who have been promoted for their technical abilities alone.

A place for psychometrics

As part of counselling, coaching or mentoring training, a useful way of creating and discussing such self-awareness aspects in a management group is found in the use of personality profiling or management style inventories. These can be used in almost any aspect of career development and performance management, from assessing new graduate recruits to providing a basis for running team development workshops.

A word of caution here is that, if the instrument is poorly administered (ie the purpose and limitations are not explained) or not fed back in a counselling way, the effect can be very destructive. People can believe a faulty interpretation more than their own experience, and this can knock their confidence. They may also become fatalistic, thinking that they are a particular 'type', and that this is set in stone. This is especially true when the difference between personality (natural inclinations) and behaviour (what you choose to do) is not properly explained (see next chapter).

Much has been published on general guidelines for the administration of psychometrics. Here are some points to consider:

Explanation of purpose and limitations

☐ Many people invest into profiling a mystique that it does not deserve. The people themselves fill in the profile, and should not be surprised if what they receive back corresponds closely with their own view of themselves. All that a profile will do is to feed back people's own preferences. These preferences are to do with the person's natural personality or inclinations, and not necessarily with their behaviour. In this sense a leopard *can* change his/her spots by learning to behave differently. Coaching will be useful here in exploring and practising some alternatives.

☐ Qualified and experienced practitioners will be aware of the need for the use of counselling skills when feeding back a questionnaire. However, there may not currently be enough emphasis on the counselling side by the test publishers or others who train people to use these tests. Typically, test publisher training involves giving the information/explanation of a particular item and then inviting comment. This is all well and good if there is an agreement on the results of the item, and you can both get into a pleasant conversation around examples of where the item has demonstrated itself in a work context. But what if we have a manager who does not agree with the item, or thinks that a particular destructive way of behaving is acceptable? Handling such a situation requires a deeper level of counselling skill than just asking a few open questions and discussing the answers. It also requires the person to be in a position to have an adult-to-adult conversation with the manager. Hence, external consultants acting as executive coaches are often called in to fulfil this role, as has been mentioned earlier.

☐ When feedback is handled internally the interpreter of the questionnaire will need to be supported by management at the most senior level both in the agreement to use such questionnaires, and in the understanding of what can ensue from feeding them back. Once again this shows the advantage of managers taking on a mentoring role as part of an organisational policy. They will also need a high degree of personal maturity and assertiveness.

☐ The use of supportive 'confronting' will be a powerful tool in this situation, as will the ability to 'reality test' using dyadic or triadic questions such as 'how do you think your direct reports view you when you . . .?' or 'how does the staff member generally react when you . . .?'

The employment of counselling skills combined with sensitive use of psychometrics can help the human resources professional to select those managers in the organisation who may make natural mentors. As such people are undoubtedly rare amongst many management populations, the use of counselling to heighten awareness of the behaviours needed, and coaching to provide the tools for change will be a powerful and effective combination.

Successful performance management will combine good systems, such as objective setting, measurement and appraisal, with an integrated approach to counselling skills. Our conviction is that the skills alone are not enough; the right relationship is vital. For this relationship to flourish, top management needs to be involved and to lend their whole-hearted support.

References

1. CLUTTERBUCK D. (1991). *Everyone Needs a Mentor.* (2nd edn.) London, Institute of Personnel and Development.
2. ROGERS C. R. (1980). *A Way of Being.* Boston MA, Houghton Mifflin.

Further reading

BLANCHARD K., ZIGARMI D. and ZIGARMI P. (1985). *Leadership and the One Minute Manager*. London, Fontana/Collins.

BLOCH S. (1993). 'Business mentoring and coaching'. *Training and Development Journal*. December, pp. 12–14.

CONWAY C. (1994). 'Mentoring managers'. *Training and Development Journal*. December, pp. 12–14.

GIBB S. (1994). 'Inside corporate mentoring schemes'. *Personnel Review*. Vol. 23, No. 3, pp. 47–60.

HAMILTON R. (1993). *Mentoring*. London, Industrial Society Press.

HUNT D. M. (1991). 'Trust: Essential to effective mentoring.' *IPM Journal*. October, pp. 29–39.

NATHAN R. and HILL L. *Career Counselling*. London, Sage.

PARSLOE E. (1995). *The Manager as Coach and Mentor*. London, Institute of Personnel and Development.

SHEA G. F. (1992). Mentoring: A guide to the basics. London, Kogan Page.

SMITH L. (1993). 'The executives' new coach'. *Fortune Magazine*. December, pp. 78–83.

WRIGHT R. G. (1991). 'Mentors at Work'. *Journal of Management Development*. Vol. 19, No. 3, pp. 25–32.

9

DESIGNING COUNSELLING SKILLS COURSES
Part One: Preparing the Ground

The scene is a counselling skills training course and the group is a mix of human resource and line managers.

'It's hot in here', someone remarked. 'Why don't we open the door?' From somewhere at the back of the room: 'Why don't we ask the door how it feels about being opened?' Sniggers and titters all round. By now the course tutor was getting puzzled as to what was going on. When the laughter died down, a hesitant and rather nervous person turned to the tutor and said, 'You know, seriously, I also attended that "self-development" programme. We kept on being asked how we felt about things to the point that it became very uncomfortable. In fact, the tutor encouraged the group to give me some un-asked for, and unwelcome "personal feedback" . . . What they said knocked my confidence and I've been living with it ever since.'

This incident is a true story, but what has it to do with designing counselling skills training courses? It illustrates how the unwitting designer of the self-development programme had created a process that was at the least highly intrusive, and at its worst potentially destructive. The remark about asking the door how it feels is illustrative of how people react when that question 'how do you feel about that?' becomes over-used. It turns a useful question into a joke . . . and as we know, humour can be a defence mechanism to ward off what is becoming uncomfortable.

Danger: tutor at work

The dangerous amateur dabbling in gratuitous self-development exercises would do well to note the British Association for Counselling's Code of Ethics. This code makes a very clear distinction between skills training and the sort of self-development training that people undergo when they become professional counsellors. Counselling skills training, when it is not designed to produce a professional counsellor at its end, serves a very different purpose. Of course, professional counsellor training also encompasses skills. However, here the focus is very much on developing the sort of self-awareness that will be essential for the long-term therapeutic relationship. This is worlds apart from the human resources or line manager in a workplace situation when a problem arises and they take on the *temporary* role of counsellor, often because they happen to be the right person in the right place, at the right time.

Human resource professionals integrate counselling skills into many functions, for example, grievance interviewing, career guidance/performance management coaching and problem solving. A model of how the HR role could fit into a wider counselling process is given in Chapter 3.

Finding themselves temporarily in the role of counsellor, their need is, therefore, for skills that will be focused on counselling the short-term problem and identifying where an issue may be beyond their skills. The process of referral has been covered earlier in this book. The idea, therefore, that the temporary counsellor needs to take on the self-development type training of the professional counsellor is not only inappropriate: it could be downright dangerous. It is essential that the basic design of the programme takes this into account.

For example, it is often safer for human resource managers to go further along the road with an issue than line managers. This is because of role conflicts both in the minds of the 'client' and of the manager. It is hard to open up to your manager, who has power to facilitate, or block, your career. It can be hard for managers to separate what may be short-term emotional problems from longer-term performance. Clients will always wonder whether what is being discussed will, one day, appear on their career record. It will take a very special manager to overcome these obstacles, but some do. Having said this, they do have a valuable role to play in recognising that someone has a problem in the first place, and not resorting immediately to disciplinary action (as outlined in Chapter 5). It is clear that, in most cases, human resource professionals should receive a different kind of training, both in depth and content, than line managers.

Preparing the ground

In this chapter we will consider some ideas and guidelines that will help to ensure that the ground is properly prepared for a training programme. We will look at how to get the balance right between skills training and self-development exercises, considering the needs of the group. We will examine what is good training practice in this situation and look at how to proceed with the aims and objectives of the programme. There is also an element of the unexpected in each programme. All groups are different because people are different; however, you can plan to take this difference into account. Finally, we will consider who should be involved in delivering the training and the kind of experience and support they will need to do so effectively.

Getting the balance right

Getting the balance right in any counselling, or indeed any interpersonal skills training, is not easy. There is a very real temptation to 'slice open' the feelings of the participants. Perhaps this is the wrong idea for the right reasons, ie to help an individual to change some unhelpful part of their behaviour. If inappropriately or badly handled, the damage may not be apparent immediately, as the story at the beginning of this chapter illustrates. The manager who had obviously been deeply affected by the feedback given on the self-development programme had derived little benefit from these revelations; quite the reverse. He had received no support or counselling following the programme that might have helped him to make use of what had been said. We often find these 'walking wounded' on our training programmes and we then have the task of picking up the pieces. Those who do not encounter a counsellor either on a course, or under other circumstances, may not be so lucky.

Melanie Child, writing in IPD's *Career Path* (the journal for the Outplacement and Career Counselling Forum), also presents a health warning about self-development programmes. She says 'there is a need for greater awareness of the pitfalls', and later in the article says 'some trainers feel that they have really achieved if one of the participants has "gone down" (become depressed by an unpleasant reality). This all too often means that the trainer has touched a raw nerve and, although potentially offering an opportunity for increased self-awareness, this may be neither the time nor the place to support such a change.'[1]

So how can the designer of a counselling skills training programme acquire the right lightness of touch? It will be helpful in the early stages of the design to take into consideration a number of issues. Once again, the important points already referred to in the BAC Code of Ethics should determine which sort of exercises should be included in the programme. Other considerations will depend upon the purpose of the programme and the specific needs of the group, and not the preferences of the trainer/designer.

The needs of the group should be respected as much as if they themselves were clients presenting themselves for counselling. After all, they are in just as vulnerable a position. This comment makes sense if we consider that professional counsellors know that part of their training is to do with personal exploration and development. The better counsellor training institutions have rigorous selection procedures that ensure trainees know what they are letting themselves in for. The unsuspecting participants of an in-company training course, however, will have no way of knowing this. They often express fears at the start of the course or in focused interviews beforehand say they think it may become too personal or intrusive (more on focused interviews later). The burden of responsibility rests with the designer/tutor to ensure that the interactions that take place will be at the right level, and appropriate for the group.

An obvious need is to make sure that time is allocated at the start of the course to explore any fears and expectations. The effect of such action will also be empowering for the group, giving the message that it is *their* course and they are in control of it. It almost goes without saying, but ploughing straight in with an assumption that you don't need to do this can be very depowering and risky.

Good training practice

All experienced trainers will be familiar with the necessary starting point for courses, ie its aims and objectives. Quite simply, we are talking about a 'horses for courses' approach where the context, ie the needs and work roles of each group, must be taken into consideration.

This approach is especially valuable when thinking about the needs of your organisation as a whole and what their expectations might be of a counselling skills programme. Very often, people in organisations are unfamiliar with counselling and may see it in a number of ways. For example, they may see it as part of a disciplinary process, or as only needed when people have personal problems and not as an integrated part of the management process, as has been mentioned before in this book. If the more proactive use of counselling skills and approaches in management practice is what you are aiming for, careful design of the aims and objectives becomes an essential part of the groundwork for the programme and, incidentally, a way of communicating what it is all about. In other words, they will help to 'sell' the programme.

From another angle, there may also be a misunderstanding that a counselling skills course will provide the company with some professional trained counsellors, and the limitations are not understood. Sometimes, counselling may be expected to solve some issues that are really to do with the systems and culture of the organisation, and the design stage may present an opportunity to make this distinction.

Focused interviews

Focused interviews are an essential part of the groundwork, and also provide a way of selling the right messages about the course. They can be done as part of a normal process of identification of training needs, and will provide you with a legitimate and non-threatening way of gathering reactions whilst, at the same time, informing people.

Examples of the kind of questions that you could ask might include:

- 'what do you see as counselling needs in this organisation?'
- 'what do you understand by the words *counselling skills?*'
- 'what do you hope will be the outcome of a counselling skills training course?'
- 'which counselling skills do you currently use?'
- 'do you see the use of counselling skills as part of day-to-day management practice?'

Naturally, the questions that you use will be specific to your own organisation. However, at the end of this process you should also be able to answer your own questions on:

- what the training course will be designed to achieve
- what the end result of the skills development will be
- what level of skill the group already has that you can build on

Most importantly, you will be designing a programme that is within the context of your organisation and will address its specific needs.

An example of the aims and objectives resulting from your focused interviews could look like this:

Aim:
- The aim of this programme is to enable the course participants to improve their counselling skills and to be better equipped to handle a range of workplace situations.

Some objectives might be:
- to be introduced to and practice some basic skills that will be helpful in workplace counselling situations
- to understand some basic models of counselling theory and how these fit in with the workplace context
- to consider the organisational culture and how this will affect the delivery of in-house counselling
- to discuss and decide when and how a counselling issue should be referred to a professional counsellor

☐ to consider both the reactive and proactive use of counselling skills and approaches.

How to plan for the unexpected

Earlier on we considered some of the pitfalls in running self-development exercises in courses. We looked at how people's emotions can be stirred up. This may be deliberate, or because of lack of knowledge and training. The nature of counselling skills training may also evoke spontaneous emotional reactions. After all, it is intrinsically about handling emotions, which is in itself an emotive subject. There will be times when people will feel vulnerable, no matter how sensitively you handle the subject matter. For some the situation can become so suddenly and unexpectedly emotionally charged that they cannot continue with a particular exercise. Even though you may have been very careful not to push people into 'self-awareness', you may find that this spontaneously occurs when you cover certain subjects.

A common example is when a discussion on bereavement counselling reminds some people of their own loss and they re-experience the grief of the past. When you then introduce a practice exercise, or role play, some people may see this as an opportunity for self-development; however, for others the situation is too raw for them to be able to continue. Good counselling skills trainers will plan for this and will be careful to respect an individual's right to opt out rather than be forced into doing something that they are not ready for.

A recommended approach would be to make the training group aware that they have a choice in this matter and to have some alternative, less threatening exercises available for those in the group who want to opt out. In this way those people who want to participate can do so, and those who do not are not sitting around twiddling their thumbs, or, more importantly, being made to feel that they have somehow failed.

Who does the training?

As we have seen, counselling skills training can be a volatile subject. No matter how safe you may try to make it, there inevitably comes a point in a course where people need to experience some kind of practice exercise in which they will be working on real issues. This is desirable because role play will only skim the surface unless real issues are involved. An important part of the training will be to help delegates to increase their sensitivity by experiencing what it feels like to be a client as well as a counsellor.

Referring once again to the BACs Code, there is a section that looks specifically at ethics and practice for trainers. It refers both to those who train people to become counsellors and those who train people in counselling skills. It is recommended that potential counselling skills trainers should read this code of ethics. However, certain issues within the code need contextualising into the workplace arena.

Two main issues stated in the code are of particular importance to the in-house trainer. These focus on issues of responsibility and issues of competence.

Responsibility and competence

When designing in-house skills courses trainers should consider that they are taking responsibility for not only the trainees, but the people who their group will be let loose on. This is why a session discussing the importance of ethical issues should be a part of the course design. The group should be made aware of their skills and their limitations when they are in counselling situations. As emphasised earlier on, the trainer is also responsible for handling the course members' own vulnerability in a professional way. Trainers need to consider their own training in relation to how deeply they can cover counselling skills and approaches with their groups.

The BAC suggests that trainers should themselves undertake a basic course in counselling training and that they should build on this with further training at regular intervals. This is, of course, a very sound idea. A further suggestion would be that they plan to run their first counselling skills training course in tandem with a more experienced person, preferably a trained counsellor, as a co-tutor. As counsellors don't necessarily make good trainers, an alternative might be having a counsellor stand by as a resource for people to talk to should they need to do so.

It is legitimate, and even desirable, for those trainers who feel themselves to be inexperienced to take this precaution of buying in a good trainer/counsellor. Acting as support tutor can be a good way of learning. An experienced trainer should be able to run a course so that it provides a 'safe' role for the support tutor. In any case, where counselling skills training is concerned two heads are better than one. Trainees will benefit from working in small, observed groups, especially in case work role-playing (see Chapter 10 for more on this).

Who counsels the trainer?

There is a strong case for counselling supervision, otherwise known as 'who counsels the counsellor' – or in this case, the trainer. This subject has been looked at earlier in this book; however, a further 'health warning' is needed. During the delivery of a course, trainers may well find themselves experiencing some of the same emotions as the trainees. All human beings have emotional experiences, some unresolved and painful. Trainers are not immune to any of this. Additionally, they have a serious responsibility to pitch the course at the right level for the group – not an easy task. For both of these reasons supervision, providing both support and a second opinion, becomes a necessity rather than a luxury. One might even say that it is a basic human right.

References

1. CHILD M. *Career Path*. London, IPD.

Further reading

BAC. (1989). Code of Ethics and Practice for Counselling Skills. Rugby, British Association for Counselling.

BRAMLEY P. (1991). *Evaluating Training Effectiveness: Translating theory into practice*. Maidenhead, McGraw-Hill.

CAREY G. (1986). *Theory and Practice of Counselling and Psychotherapy*. (3rd edn.) Monterey CA, Brooks Cole.

INSTITUTE OF PERSONNEL AND DEVELOPMENT. *The IPD Statement on Counselling in the Workplace.* London, IPD.

MEGGINSON D. and PEDLER M. (1992). *Self-development: A facilitator's guide.* Maidenhead, McGraw Hill.

SUMMERFIELD J. (1995). 'Ethical coniderations: counselling at work.' BAC. No. 8, pp. 5–6.

10

DESIGNING COUNSELLING SKILLS COURSES
Part Two: Choosing the Right Menu

In Chapter 9 we considered essential programme preparation. Provided that this groundwork has been done, choosing the right content should be easier, because the context has been clarified.

Trainers will need to consider the methods that they will employ. These will almost certainly include participative methods such as role-play, syndicate group work and the perhaps less familiar interpersonal process recall. Trainers will also need to be aware of how a particular group is reacting at any time: what is often called group dynamics. Counselling is a very practical subject and input on theory alone is not enough. More on this later.

The methods presented in this chapter will be suitable both for counselling skills courses and for other courses that include such skills, for example, performance management, team development, and managing change. However, a clear distinction will be drawn between short course training and the type of training that professional counsellors undertake.

Linking with the models and skills presented in Chapter 4 we will consider how to integrate these into your courses.

General guidelines for running short courses

The hero of Nikos Kazantzakis' novel *Zorba the Greek* illustrates an important point about how personal learning occurs. He exhibits clear personal preferences for trying to understand new information in this conversation:

'Everything, men, animals, trees, stars; we are all one substance involved in some terrible struggle.' Zorba scratched his
head and said, 'I've got a thick skull, boss, I don't grasp these
things easily. Ah, if only you could dance all that you've just
said, then I'd understand . . . or if you could tell me all that in
a story.'

Viewing and listening are both acceptable to Zorba, but he
prefers abstract ideas to be made concrete, and ideas to be presented through action. Counselling skills training works best
when the learning is just as Zorba describes it: action-centred.
It is about experiencing how the use of skills can create better
working relationships as well as solving short-term emotional
problems. The minimum of theory with the maximum practice: counselling is not an academic subject.

In this context the leading of role-plays and other practical
exercises become a vital area to address.

Suggested methods for role-play exercises

Role-play situations in counselling and counselling skills training are often arranged around the notion of working in triads;
one person role-playing the client, one the counsellor/helper,
and the third person in the observer position. Triads work effectively as long as attention is given to a number of important
points, not the least of which is role clarity.

Each person of the three needs to be clear about what they
are doing at any one time. To help this happen it is important
that each party is given a clear written brief and adequate
time to prepare. In the situation where detailed case work is
being practised, plenty of time for preparation should be
allowed, perhaps briefing the delegates overnight and then getting them to prepare in pairs the next day to encourage the
sharing of ideas. This can easily be managed if you are divid-
ing the group into two or three smaller sub-groups with the
same brief. People can then prepare with the person who has
their corresponding brief in another group. If there is a particular brief that rings a bell for the role player, raising the issue
at this early stage can prevent a later problem.

We have found that the more time that is given for preparation, the more confident the group participants will feel about

the role-play and the more effective it will be in terms of a learning experience.

The observer role

The observer is in an ideal position to give feedback to the 'counsellor', being a person who has worked with this group member throughout the duration of the programme, and as a peer colleague their feedback may be seen as having a value separate from the feedback given by the 'expert' tutor. If the peer member, who is not an expert, can easily see the use of skills, then the 'counsellor' can be sure that they are using the skills in a clear way. Usually the observer holds the time boundaries and he or she must indicate when it is time to stop one activity and start another. Finally, observing a role-play can be at least as valuable an experience for the observer as it is for the 'counsellor'. Observing is another way of reinforcing learning.

The client role

The person playing the client has the responsibility for providing the best possible opportunity for the trainee counsellor to practise. The tutor should make it clear that this is the main purpose of the role-play. It should not be taken as an opportunity for the client to 'dump' emotionally on the counsellor ie using it as an opportunity to find relief by spilling out a real, but too 'heavy' problem. The new learner could feel swamped and seriously put off by this experience.

Should the role-play contain an issue which is currently live and painful for the person role-playing the client to act out, the tutor should intervene. The client needs to be given time to decide whether to carry on, or withdraw from the exercise rather than be drawn inappropriately into their own emotional material. It is the tutor's task to ensure that this is a normal part of the process of learning and to see to it that course members will not feel like failures for having withdrawn from the role-play. It is important, therefore, that the person playing the client can stick closely to the brief (another reason for good preparation).

The client should not, on the other hand, collude with the 'counsellor' to make anything plain sailing, nor should he or she be deliberately obstructive. Because people vary in their ability to carry out the client role, tutors observing role-plays should be prepared to allow the 'counsellor' a second attempt at a role-play if they have not been given a good chance to practise the skills by the client.

Sometimes, people playing the client role become so wrapped up in it that the other course members think that the issue being practised is real. We can all be touched by genuine emotions when acting out scenarios that contain commonly painful human experiences. In these cases, it may be necessary for the tutor to offer the person playing the client the opportunity to 'de-role', not only for their own sake, but because they may be anxious that the rest of the group thinks that they have a problem that they do not, in fact, have. This can be done by offering the client the opportunity to say out loud something like, 'I am (insert real name) not (insert role-play name) and these problems are really not mine, I was just acting them out'.

The counsellor role

The 'counsellor', via the role-play scenario, acts out the new learning for the triad. He or she has a responsibility to ask for feedback in as open and non-defensive a way as possible. To aid learning from role-plays that occur early on in a course, and to provide skills practice, the tutor may encourage the 'counsellor' to concentrate on two or three learning points and ask for feedback only on these. Such one-bite-at-a-time learning is effective for all new skills acquisition. Aside from this, as with the other two roles, the 'counsellor' should study the brief carefully and stick to directions.

In all role-play situations tutors should be available to answer questions during preparation time and to explain learning points as many times as is needed. Role-playing is, after all, just another opportunity to practise, and the better that the group does in its practice sessions, the more confident you will feel to let them loose on real clients.

Triads for use without role-play

Triads (groups of three) may be used in a similar way when the practice sessions call for the course members to work on their own material. This will be appropriate in cases where deeper skills training is taking place, for example with groups from HR, welfare and occupational health. The learning intention is for the course member to experience what it feels like to be in the client's shoes, ie to divulge real information about themselves. The specific purpose of such an exercise is to develop sensitivity.

Discretion on the issues and level of self-disclosure is best left to the person being the client (the rule of no gratuitous 'dumping' still, of course, applies). A useful idea to help the group to select a subject to talk about that is real and yet feels OK is to create a list of 'safe' topics from which they can select an appropriate subject. For example, the contents of this list could contain lighter subjects that still have some personal content, eg 'I should take more exercise' or 'If I won the National Lottery . . .' or, perhaps, 'managing home and work demands' – a heavier subject but still safe for most people to choose the level of disclosure that they wish to make.

On the subject of handling feedback, IPR, or interpersonal process recall, is a useful tool for all methods of learning feedback and is worth some exploration. Combined with the use of a video tape, which the trainee can view and keep, it will serve as a long-term reminder of the learning.

Interpersonal process recall

This is a method for individual self-learning, or a 'self-discovery process'. It is part of a method called 'tutor personal process recall'. It is suitable for every level of skills training because it can be adapted in depth and quality to suit the particular learning group. This is a judgement that each tutor must make for each group that they train.

In any interaction we may pick up messages, or cues, from the other person, some of which we may be only half-aware of. Feelings, thoughts and bodily reactions flash through at great speed. Some of these we suppress, some puzzle us, some we communicate to the other person and we are probably only half-conscious of what is going on inside of us.

Replaying an audio or video tape can help to gain access to such hidden information. A good learning method here is to allow the person who was being recorded to stop the tape themselves to discuss a particular point of learning, with the tutor giving only supplementary input from time to time, or if an important point has been overlooked.

This process can help to develop three specific points of learning:

1 To help the trainee to develop their skills and understand the thoughts and feelings that they were experiencing during the practice session. Giving the person the opportunity to comment themselves on their own performance allows for a high degree of choice and control over the process. This models the relationship that people should have with their clients, ie not taking control but helping the client to work out their problems for themselves; empowering, not depowering, them.

2 To help the other trainees to learn from example and to participate in the feedback process.

3 To increase the trainees' self-awareness in a safe way, ie by facilitating constructive and focused feedback that is not of the gratuitous 'self-awareness' type of exercise referred to in Chapter 9. This way of handling feedback promotes awareness in relation to the skills that are being practised and gives the trainee ideas on how they should handle things the next time around. As such it leaves no loose ends for the person to brood over, in a way that we have seen can be very destructive to their level of confidence.

The tutor's role in facilitating interpersonal process recall
We have considered some methods for feedback on learning points for practice sessions, with and without the use of video. It may be useful, for the tutor facilitator who is less experienced in these situations, to consider how to lead the feedback in terms of their own and the group's interventions.

Here are some guidelines:

☐ Use exploratory, brief, open-ended questions.
☐ Encourage a focus on the use of skills and the processes occurring, not on personal comments about the person themselves.

☐ Focus on the video tape, then rather than now. This allows the person to own that they are viewing the past and that they are able to move on to improve on their performance in the future.

The following questions have been found to be useful in promoting a constructive discussion on both the skills and the processes, ie internal thoughts and feelings and the counselling relationship:

'How were you responding at that moment?'
'What do you think the other person was thinking and feeling?'
'Which skills were you aware of using?'
'Did you have any plans about where you wanted the session to go?'
'Was there anything that you wanted to say, but could not find the appropriate words?'
'Was the other person giving you any clues about the way that they were thinking or feeling?'
'What did you do that you were pleased about?'
'Was there anything that was difficult for you?'
'Was there anything that you would like to do differently next time?'
'What have you learned from this practice session?'

Group dynamics

We need to consider the group as a whole, not just individuals within it. Many trainers will be familiar with the fact that all learning groups take on a shape and form of behaviour that has been called 'group dynamics'. This also occurs in groups undertaking counselling skills training, to a lesser or greater extent, depending on the depth of the training.

We will look at dynamics in the specific context of counselling skills training, linking the theory with some practical ideas.

The learning stages of the group and group dynamics

Learning groups in counselling skills training typically move through a number of stages. Descriptions of these stages vary from three, to seven or eight.

As with all maps and models they are not set in concrete and all groups will have a different 'life' and go through different processes. However, they are useful as a guideline. For example, some groups will pass quickly through some stages, or they can get stuck in a particular one. If this occurs then knowledge of the stages, and the processes linked with each, can be invaluable to the tutor. In Chapter 9 we considered that course leaders need to be both responsible and competent and each trainer must judge themselves in the light of their own training and experience and that of their group. It is unlikely, however, that delegates on a short course will progress further than the very early stages of group development.

It is important to know that there are some sensitive issues for the tutor, as well as the group, in counselling skills training. The course leader can influence or block the group's learning process. For example, if tutors are not comfortable with emotional issues they may not allow an open and mature discussion.

One of the best known and appropriate theories is Tuckman's 'forming, storming, norming and performing' which is based on a review of some 50 studies of group development.

Stages of group development

Stage one – forming. Here the group is orientating to the task which will include discovering the nature of the task, its boundaries, exchanging information, and perhaps expressing uncertainty by grumbling about the setting, suspicion, and the seeking of rules and procedures. There is also a period of testing and dependence where they will test their relationship with the tutor or leader, and with each other. This will include decisions about whether to join or not to join, attempts to structure the group, and hesitant participation.

In counselling skills training

The tutor should work hard at the start of the programme to help the group to form supportive relationships. Any early contributions by members should be positively reinforced. This can be achieved by:

- [ ] asking the group to 'brainstorm' their hopes and fears about the course
- [ ] setting up a 'contract' of confidentiality, ie that what happens in the group stays within the four walls of the training room
- [ ] adopting an adult-to-adult approach, ie not being parental, or over-controlling with the group. This sets the scene for the group to feel in control of their own course. Groups who feel relaxed and trust their tutor will share more easily
- [ ] keeping things 'safe' for the group by preparing the ground, as described in Chapter 9.

Stage two – storming. As the group moves on into the course it may exhibit emotional responses to tasks that they may be seen as 'demanding', for example, challenging the validity of the task; ambivalence towards the leader; and even aggression if the task requires high personal commitment and some self-disclosure. Some intra-group conflict might occur, such as defensiveness; competition; jealousy; cliques and factions forming and then breaking up; and general disruption and frustration.

In counselling skills training
- [ ] Unlike professional counsellor training, groups rarely get into the storming stage.
- [ ] Although it may spontaneously happen, there is no usefulness in facilitating storming on short courses where it does not form part of a longer-term relationship, as in professional training. More on this later.
- [ ] If you see that the group is getting defensive ask yourself what could be happening to cause this, back off, and then ask the group. It is empowering for a group to have the control left with them in this way. You are demonstrating that you will not push them further than they are willing to go.

Stage three – norming. The storming phase can be seen as the members of the groups attempt to become 'adult' and interpret things for themselves. In the norming stage the group will often ask for opinions, give opinions, express feelings constructively and evaluate these feelings and opinions in relation to the task. In this stage a 'group consciousness' develops where members co-operate and support each other, individual boundaries are established and respected (ie what each person will or won't talk about and reveal about themselves) and conflict generally reduces, with harmony on the increase.

In counselling skills training

☐ Groups that contain a high proportion of mature, confident people often pass over the storming stage and exhibit norming behaviour.

☐ Less confident groups may start to exhibit such behaviours only towards the end of a programme. Our experience is that it takes at least three days for groups to become comfortable and confident with each other.

☐ Groups may not naturally be aware of and respect each other's boundaries. The role of the tutor here is to notice when an individual's boundaries are being overstepped and gently to curtail the process.

Stage four – performing. Insight and understanding are the keynotes to this stage. Solutions emerge from the group as tasks are dealt with, unfettered by personal difficulties. The asking and giving of suggestions, rather than opinions, occurs and there is pragmatic support of the tasks.

In counselling skills training

☐ The question here is how short is a short course? We have found that groups that are together for five days or more often move into the performing stage, gaining more insight daily.

☐ There is a strong case here for follow-up case work, with group supervision being a normal part of the training. Groups which come back together, having counselled real clients, show greater insight and understanding and begin to 'hypothesise' for themselves about what the issues might be with their clients.

☐ Because the training is not as thorough, or as long, as professional training, individuals may find that they encounter a personal difficulty that they had not expected when they practise the skills in real situations. Their performance is greatly enhanced if they can discuss these difficulties in case-work meetings, and work with the referral process.

Having looked at these possible processes we need to consider what course leaders can do to help the group to learn, and also what will hinder their development. Once again, a mature trainer will decide how easy, or difficult, it will be to do any or all of this.

What helps the group to develop?
☐ the willingness to be process-orientated, ie to understand how it is working and what it is doing
☐ the willingness to be interactive, ie to give and receive feedback, receive impressions, share thoughts and ideas about your own learning
☐ the willingness to challenge the group supportively, ie to resolve conflicts and to keep the boundaries for individuals.

What hinders group development?
☐ narrowness in learning, ie the group is limited to one kind of educational experience when the tutor is only willing to be didactic or provide all of the input from 'the platform'
☐ cultural oppression, ie any negative values and beliefs existing in the organisational culture seep into the group, and the tutor is not willing to let the group explore different norms and values, or to make comparisons
☐ psychological defensiveness, ie bad past experiences cause the group to be anxious about the present and the tutor will need to work hard to overcome these fears and to make the group feel safe. In this case trust needs to be developed; the seat of control needs to be with the group. Self-awareness and disclosure will be particularly threatening and the course leader will need to be sensitive in their choice of tasks.

Professional counsellor training

Professional counsellor training would include challenging individuals in the group about the effect of their behaviour, and how they are reacting to each other. This would form an important part of developing self-awareness. Counsellors are 'aware' on two levels when they are with clients. They work with what the client is saying and doing, and also with their own reactions and 'gut feel' about what is going on. The better institutions will make trainees go into personal counselling themselves as a necessary part of the training.

In contrast to the creation of the 'safe environment' on short courses, professional training involves some risk. Part of the development process will be to work through unresolved emotional issues and delegates will be encouraged to discuss openly what they are feeling when they hit a sensitive subject. This will ensure that they are not surprised by their emotions when they are counselling their clients. This contrasts with the temporary counsellor, who is encouraged to refer the person on if their own emotions interfere with the process. Course colleagues will be encouraged to support and counsel each other. Groups become much closer and their relationships are a legitimate part of the learning, called 'group process' or 'experiential learning'.

Professional training will usually contain much more input on theory. For example, counsellors cannot work with the process of 'transference', when it arises, if they do not recognise it in the first place.

These are just some of the key differences that exist, and a consideration of them will be useful in helping trainers running short courses to develop the right lightness of touch.

Models and skills

In Chapter 4 we looked at some models and assessed their application to the workplace. We also considered the skills that are linked with useful models, such as the Egan three-stage approach. Clearly, it would be unwise for a tutor working with non-professional counsellors to build in exercises around the more advanced techniques associated with some models. Some of these present complex and subtle aspects of client–counsellor relationships: the counselling process.

A starting-point in the training of temporary counsellors should always be skills not processes. People can get their hands around skills, they are easily understood and they build confidence in the group. Watching people who have just discovered reflecting and tried it for the first time can be a revelation. At first it is uncomfortable, it's new and unlike anything that they have tried before. As they begin to realise the effectiveness of it, as they see their clients opening up and finding their own expression for their problem, the feeling is one of relief. 'I can do this after all . . . I can acquire the skills and behaviours.'

Because the skills will be a mixture of the familiar and the new, the training should be built around small chunks of input, followed by practice sessions. Familiar skills may be open questions or summarising. New ones will be reflecting and circular questions, eg dyadic or triadic.

The range of exercises can include small group, or syndicate discussion; paired discussion using 'what would you do if . . . ?' scenarios; case-work discussion and practice; and, of course, observer group role-play. A powerful source of learning for groups can be periodic tutor demonstrations where the group sees the skills that they have been practising come together in a 'live' situation. We have found that training videos rarely match the effectiveness of this method.

Making the group aware that there are processes and relationships that happen in counselling also serves some useful purposes. It can heighten the group's acceptance of their own limitations and of the need for referral. Our experience has been that groups show great relief on hearing that it is OK to have limitations, and that referral is both necessary and desirable. 'You mean I don't have to handle *everything* that comes up in a counselling session . . . ?'

Continuous development

Finally, developing counselling skills is not a process that ends with the last day of a course. Those of us who have been through professional training know that the learning never ends. The issues are as varied as the numbers of people presenting them. We know our limitations, but can push out our boundaries as we go on to greater depth and experience. We do this with the safety net of a good supervisor, whose greater experience and ability to stand back from the situation always proves to be invaluable.

For human resource and line managers, there is always the choice to stay with the skills they have learned, and be comfortable with their own limitations. They can also choose to continue their training and take on a more professional counselling role, and some do.

Further reading and listening

ACHESON F. and LAKER A. (1990). *A Counselling Listener.* (Audio tapes.) Cambridge, National Extension College.

EGAN G. (1990). *The Skilled Helper.* Monteray CA, Brooks Cole.

INSKIPP F. and JOHNS H. *Principles of Counselling Series I and II.* (Audio tapes.) St Leonards-on-Sea, Alexia Publications.

KAGAN N. (1976). *Interpersonal Process Recall.* Michigan MI, Michigan State University.

STEWART J. T. (1989). *The Helper's Handbook.* Cambridge, National Extension College.

11

USING COUNSELLING
SKILLS PROACTIVELY:
The Bottom Line

In each of the chapters of this book we have looked at the nature of counselling skills and approaches in a workplace context. Whilst it is clear that such approaches are needed where people-problems exist, they can also prevent such problems occurring in the first place. We have demonstrated that they have an integrated place in the overall well-being of the organisation as well as of the individuals within it. What is at stake is nothing less than efficiency and effectiveness and, ultimately, business success.

Because no strategy can really work without the commitment of the top people in an organisation, the issue also becomes one of leadership. As someone once said, 'Leadership is a word so soaked with meaning that we can wring almost anything we want out of it.' However we define it, one thing is clear: successful people-management depends on creating a relationship and a set of skills that can be learned. For many managers this learning curve is uncomfortably steep. For example, in situations where they are promoted for their technical ability alone it is likely that their focus will be on tasks rather than people. These may be seen as 'hard' skills, and good people-management behaviours as 'soft' skills, ie not really necessary for the success of the business. Where managers do see the connection between their relationship with their people and organisational success, they often lack the wherewithal to turn good intentions into actions.

Counselling the organisation
As we said at the outset of this book, counselling has been drawn into organisations by such needs as handling outplacement,

stress, post-raid trauma, the survivor syndrome; a retroactive application. The challenge is how to become proactive. The search is on for the right system or process to help to effect changes in the business. The empowerment machine is an example of this, and we have stated that we see counselling as the 'oil'. Proactive or preventive strategies seem to have taken root in some organisations in the USA, and we will examine at least one large organisation's experience.

Winning hearts and minds

Whatever we say about the pace of change in the last decade, we can all at least agree that human beings do not easily accept change, even change for the better. We have suggested that really effective change management programmes seem to be few and far between. Those that do succeed, we further suggest, are built on counselling skills and approaches.

A very relevant piece of UK research has been carried out by Peter Herriot and Carole Pemberton.[1] In their book, Herriot and Pemberton research into the kinds of contract or *mutually beneficial relationships* between organisations and managers/professionals. Researching over the last two decades, they found that the contract used to imply mutual commitment and trust over the long term, but that is now in the past. Herriot and Pemberton feel that a new contract is called for that meets the needs both of individuals and organisations. We agree, and once again we put the emphasis squarely on the need for new relationships, not just new business systems.

Knowledge and trust

Alan M. Webber, reporting in the *Harvard Business Review*, takes stock of the last decade and discusses the predictions that business observers have been making about the coming of a 'new economy' in the USA. He says:

> In the knowledge economy, the most important work is conversation – and creating trust is the manager's most important job.[2]

Webber goes on to say that 'for more and more managers who have been witnessing recent changes in their world, that new economy clearly has arrived.' Although Webber refers to American corporations such as General Motors, IBM and Sears, the issues are disturbingly familiar to a British ear, for example:

> Across the corporate landscape, in every industry and at every level, managers are struggling to adapt to unfamiliar circumstances and new strains of competition . . . the remedies at hand make up a familiar menu of corporate change: total quality management, continuous improvement, down sizing, outsourcing, business process re-engineering, focusing on core competencies and capabilities. The same set of programmes is proliferating at nearly every company.

What Webber is saying is that 'companies may embrace a "change process" but still not change the essence of the company.' *Such change processes are then in danger of becoming a cosmetic exercise.* He writes in the context of the 'new economy', but what he says strikes a chord that rings true for the UK; '. . . managing the new economy requires not just change programmes but *a changed mindset*'. This mindset, he suggests, is the belief in the vital importance of one thing: trust. His suggestion is that the creation of the sort of environment that will allow a flow of learning and knowledge is based on trust and 'conversation', ie the sharing of the knowledge, skills and concepts that create an organisation. More specifically they 'create and express the emotional environment of the company . . . they reveal who we are to others . . . they depend on bedrock human qualities; authenticity, character, integrity . . .'[3]

Such words sound familiar to a counselling ear in that they echo those qualities inherent in a counselling approach, ie respect, empathy and genuinness behaviours that we have visited before in this book. There is no short-cut to trust. No magic wand can be waved to create it. Once again, it starts with the willingness to embrace new ways of behaving and new working relationships.

Tom Peters well understands the importance of trust as an essential ingredient. He calls it 'the missing X Factor', yet Webber strikes another chord when he says 'what is difficult – and what Peters does not do – is to provide an honest and tough-minded evaluation of why *fear* tends to dominate so many organisations, why trust is so hard to achieve and so fragile to maintain'. His suggestion is that trust does not happen, essentially because managers fear the price involved in creating trust – that price being the willingness to be vulnerable, to face and resolve conflict and to live with ambiguity. The universal management tradition is to be, as Webber puts it 'steeped in rationalism, hierarchies, rule-based decision-making and authority based on titles.'[4] Above all, the threat to managers is that of loss of control.

So what does all of this boil down to? It is this: no change can take place without some human adjustments, some of which might be painful. No fine new glossy mission statement alone can achieve change. Superficial programmes get superficial responses. The need is for approaches that will not just define new values and behaviours, important as these things are, but will win people's willingness to translate these behaviours into their own day-to-day working actions. The questions for them will be: What does this mean for me? Where do I fit in? What do I need to continue doing/do more of/do less of? Will I lose anything by doing this? Internal personal change is what makes change management really work . . . and personal change is what counselling is all about.

The question now becomes one of how all of this can be achieved. What are the processes through which meaningful and lasting change can occur?

Melting down the jelly: a starting-point

A story comes to mind. It is about a conversation that took place between a consultant business psychologist and a managing director who was grappling with how he could effect change in his company. The MD was saying, 'Every Saturday I see my people going off to the football ground and giving their all for their team. I'm not asking for much, just a little bit of that enthusiasm.' 'Well,' came the reply, 'I took my children to a party the other day and I was reminded of your organisation.' Surprised reaction. 'At the party they had a jelly mould in the shape of a rabbit and this triggered a thought. Think of your organisation as having a certain shape and that you need to change this shape to achieve success. You will need to find a way of creating a new shape. Just dropping another mould over the top, say in the shape of a lion, just won't work. People will *say* that they are lions but still *act* like rabbits! As long as the jelly is still set it will remain a rabbit. First you have to *melt down* the jelly.'

What was being said in this memorable explanation was that people's thoughts and emotions, views, ideas and doubts about change need to be ventilated before any real change can take place. They need to feel that it is safe to express views and doubts, safe to ask for help in developing whatever skills, behaviours, knowledge and personal change is needed to make things work for them. If these safe conditions can be created they will experience trust. The process itself creates the end result that this MD was after: enthusiasm and commitment.

The means by which this melting down, in order to reshape, can be achieved are neither superficial nor cosmetic. Lasting change results when all people agree to a small step in the right direction rather than paying lip-service to a few powerful people at the top. A 1 per cent change in everyone is better than a 100 per cent change in a few. Sensitively facilitated groups where such ventilation can take place and new behaviours agreed are just a starting-point along the road to change; embedding change into an organisation is a long-term process. Below are some other starting-points where a counselling approach can make a difference.

Pulling together
The senior management team need to all be singing from the same hymn sheet. One powerful dissenter can sabotage a programme. When GE in the USA changed its culture, with outstandingly successful results, those who insisted on hanging on to hierarchical, control-driven management behaviours were asked to offer their resignation. In a statement to shareholders, the Chairman of GE said, 'What we are looking for today at GE are leaders at every level who can energise, excite and coach rather than enervate, depress and control.'

As we mentioned earlier, from facilitated groups, at all levels of the organisation, new behaviours can emerge. Group events also provide an opportunity to pick up on managers who may be struggling with change. Individual counselling can be very potent in such cases, where managers may be blocked by emotional needs that are in conflict with the new culture. Often such people are not the most senior managers but the middle managers who have fought their way up the ladder and for whom a higher position was hard to come by. To lose such managers would be a waste, because they would take their experience and knowledge of the organisation with them. Sadly, in many organisations where managers do not fit, for any reason, their loss is often seen as the only viable option.

In the UK the sharing of control, usually by middle managers, is associated with a particular process: that of empowerment. This is worth examining.

Because of the sensitive nature of change work, external consultants are invariably brought in to support both the group and individual processes. At the early stages the needs are for an assurance of confidentiality and the establishing of credibility for the programme. In the long term, by far the greater benefit will be felt when the members of the organisation own the process themselves. Senior managers and human resource professionals will score points with their people by being seen to shoulder both the difficult as well as the fun aspects of the programme. Perhaps consultants who are appropriately trained and qualified can provide the best service to organisations by being willing to transfer their skills and to train change-management project leaders.

Counselling and empowerment

The concept of empowerment has been, and still is, a strong driving philosophy in many public- and private-sector organisations throughout the USA, UK, and globally. However, there is ambivalence about the word and few people have a really clear idea of what empowerment means. Many change management programmes in the UK include a move towards empowering employees, and our conviction is that successful empowerment will be rooted in counselling skills and approaches.

Sometimes the word itself can create intense emotional tension when it is used, disreputably, to mean more work with less time to do it and for less money. In these situations we have seen that the very use of the word creates a wave of negative feelings throughout an organisation. Furthermore, what stands in the way of success are issues to do with motivations and uncertainty, especially among middle managers, who play a vital role.

The Industrial Society's survey *Managing Best Practice* devotes a whole issue to the subject and focuses on transitions that are needed in both thought and feelings:

> Empowerment is far more than delegation. It is based on the belief that to be successful, organisations must harness the creativity and the brain power of all their employees – not just a few managers. The ramifications of this fundamental shift in thinking are widely underestimated and not fully understood by many organisations. Some empowerment initiatives have as a consequence stalled or fizzled out – leading to employees' feeling let down and suspicious. Once this has happened it is extremely difficult to restart the initiative.

Further on in the issue it says:

> Managers at all levels must be given the *training, coaching, help, and support* [our italics] to change role. Some managers will readily accept the benefits of empowering the workforce but others will just as readily resist it. Many got to where they are by command and control skills and are likely to revert to these behaviours, particularly where they are under pressure.[5]

Even when they are not under pressure, managers may give out mixed messages because they have mixed feelings about sharing their power. It is hard for a manager who has fought his or her way up the ladder suddenly to relinquish control if he or she can see nothing of benefit that will replace it. This will be exacerbated by any self-esteem problems and fears about letting go of control. This especially applies to middle managers who, according to *Managing Best Practice*, 'are most likely to be hostile to it'. The changes they experience the most difficulty with are:

☐ more emphasis on supporting staff, rather than controlling
☐ more emphasis on training and developing staff

- more emphasis on communication
- more of a personnel role.

Clearly, middle managers need both group and individual support if they are going to change. They will also need something specific to replace what they are giving up. Careful attention needs to be given to what this might be. An example could be combining career development initiatives with a newly created financial reward system.

This does not mean to say that we should assume that with senior managers it is all plain sailing. The major issue with top managers is that they are unused to receiving feedback on their style and practices. In some organisations a managing director inviting such behaviour towards him- or herself would be viewed as a failure. Invested in the job title is the implication that, by now, they should be all-seeing and all-knowing – an unreasonable but common assumption. So what specifically do we mean by a counselling approach in the context of empowerment?

Casting out the mote

In counselling, the sign of health in a relationship is the client's ability honestly to examine themselves and to feel empowered to effect change in their lives. This is also the sign of a healthy organisation. So here is a test: how does your organisation rate on the following three behaviours?

Congruence Otherwise known as genuineness or honesty, congruence is a word that has been used much in this book in the context of the counselling relationship. The relationship is powerful and, therefore, could be manipulative in the wrong hands. People resent being manipulated. So whether you are in a senior position or an HR manager, ask yourself:

- Do you promise more than you give? By 'empowerment' does your organisation mean more work for less money?
- By 'culture change' does it mean mass redundancies?
- Does your organisation invite and receive feedback, even at the highest level, from your people on what is, and what is not, working well in the organisation?

Relationships The counselling relationship is one of equality and trust. Sound familiar? The sense that one has with a good counsellor is of being partners on an unknown journey. A good counsellor will help interpret where you have travelled, the nature of your journey and where new steps will lead. So, some questions about relationships:

☐ Does your organisation share with its people past and future strategies?

☐ Do your people have a strong sense of being included in their own futures?

☐ Are your people openly invited to add their own ideas and knowledge to business strategies?

☐ On a micro-level, do your people participate in decisions affecting how they carry out their own jobs?

Emotional blocks The issues that block self-power in clients who receive counselling are often to do with low self-esteem, fear of change, lack of assertiveness and depression (feelings of helplessness). We focus on senior managers because they have the power to make or break new initiatives. Managers at all levels have the same issues as the rest of the population and are often stuck for ways to resolve them, for reasons we have already outlined. The questions for organisations are:

☐ Does your organisation create a safe, confidential process where both managers and their teams can be counselled about their hopes and fears?

☐ Do you have performance management or career development processes that hold water well enough for managers to find a route into such support?

☐ Are senior managers who are over-controlling challenged about their style, or are they allowed to sabotage the processes of change and empowerment?

The last word: enlightened self-interest

Integration is the key. When this happens, counselling skills and approaches create a mutual learning process. We believe that this will add value to the bottom line and, as we said earlier in this book, any new management system will fall short of expectations if relationships are ignored. To quote the chairman of General Electric:

> The highest compliment you could give GE managers a few years ago was to say that they were 'on top of things' or had 'gotten their arms around them'. These techniques, more useful in *tackling* people than coaching them, are difficult to get rid of. What we are looking for today at GE are managers who can energise, excite and coach, rather than enervate, depress and control. And never has this atmosphere been more critical. Today *everyone* must be *engaged* if we are to win. The kind of people that we need in this company are those unwilling to 'put in their time' in the bowels of the bureaucracy, or grunt along under the heel of some autocrat for years before they get the chance to make decisions, try something and be rewarded in their souls as well as their wallets [our italics].

GE changed a lot organisationally in its reward systems and management structures, becoming more 'boundaryless'. The key issue of breaking down the barriers to good relationships was vital to success: radical changes for a radical result. Significantly, the words 'counselling', or 'counselling approaches' are never used, although it is clear that genuineness, empathy and respect have been important ingredients in the process.

In the UK, the time is right for something new to happen between organisations and their employees. Counselling skills and approaches can create the new relationships that will be essential to successful change. We might then ask whether it is time that counselling ceased to be the 'C' word in organisations, and its value at last understood. Perhaps the embracing of the word in itself will be seen as a sign of health.

References

1. HERRIOT P. and PEMBERTON C. (1995). *New Deals*. Bognor Regis, John Wiley and Sons.
2. WEBBER A. M. (1993). 'What's new about the new economy?' *Harvard Business Review*. January–February, pp. 4–12.
3. *Ibid.*

4. *Ibid.*
5. THE INDUSTRIAL SOCIETY. (1995). 'Empowerment.' *Managing Best Practice.* Vol. 8, February.

Further reading

ALPANDER G. C. (1991). 'Developing managers' ability to empower employees'. *Journal of Management Development.* Vol. 10, No. 3, pp. 13–24.

EGAN G. (1993). 'The shadow side.' *Management Today.* September, pp. 32–8.

HARDINGHAM A. (1992). *Making Change Work for You.* London, Sheldon Business Books.

HERZBERG F. (1966). *Work and the Nature of Man.* New York, Word Books.

– (1973). 'One more time: how do you motivate employees?' *Harvard Business Review.* January–February, pp. 53–62.

JACKSON P. R. (1993). 'The reactions of those who survive lay-offs: a digest of recent research.' *International Journal of Selection and Assessment.* Vol. 1, No. 4, pp. 244–6.

PICKARD J. (1994). 'Empowerment in organisations.' *Personnel Management.* May.

RIPLEY R. E. and RIPLEY M. J. (1993). 'Empowerment: what to do with troubling employees? *Journal of Managerial Psychology.* Vol. 8, No. 3, pp. 3–9.

SUMMERFIELD J. (1993). 'Counselling and the concept of empowerment.' *Career Path.* London, Institute of Personnel Management, winter, pp. 3–4.

APPENDICES

Appendix 1

NATIONAL COUNSELLING AND ADVISORY ORGANISATIONS

General

British Association for Counselling
1 Regent Place
Rugby
Warwickshire CV2 2PJ

Tel: 01788 550899

A national body providing information about counselling services and individual counsellors.

Ageing

Age Concern England
Astral House
1268 London Road
London SW16 4ER

Tel: 0181 679 8000

A national network of local groups serving the needs of the elderly.

AIDS

Terrence Higgins Trust
52/54 Gray's Inn Road
London WC1X 8JU

Tel: 0171 242 1010

National organisation providing advice and information on Acquired Immune Deficiency Syndrome.

Alcohol

Alcoholics Anonymous
PO Box 1
Stonebow House
Stonebow
York
North Yorkshire YO1 2NJ

Tel: 01904 644026

A network of support groups for those with alcohol and drug problems.

Bereavement

CRUSE
Cruse House
126 Sheen Road
Richmond
Surrey TW9 1UR

Tel: 0181 940 4818/7227

Counselling and practical advice for those who are bereaved or suffering from terminal illness. Local branches.

Depression

Fellowship of Depressives Anonymous
36 Chestnut Avenue
Beverley
Humberside HU17 9QU

Tel: 01482 860619

Network of support groups for those suffering from depression.

Drugs and Alcohol

Narcotics Anonymous
PO Box 417
London SW10 0RP

Tel: 0171 498 9005

Turning Point
CAP House
9/12 Long Lane
London EC1A 9HA

Tel: 0171 606 3947

Both organisations offering advice, rehabilitation and care to alcohol and drug abusers, their families and friends.

Eating disorders

The Maisner Centre for Eating Disorders
PO Box 464
Hove
East Sussex BN3 3UG

Tel: 01273 729818 (answerphone)

One-to-one telephone consultation for bulimia and compulsive eating disorders.

Eating Disorders Association
Sackville Place
44 Magdalen Street
Norwich NR3 1JE

Tel: 01603 621414/619090

Provides information literature and a network of self-help groups.

Family and Marriage Problems

National Family Conciliation Council
Shaftesbury Centre
Percy Street
Swindon
Wiltshire SN2 2AZ

Tel: 01793 514055

Relate: National Marriage Guidance
Herbert Gray College
Little Church Street
Rugby
Warwickshire CV21 3AP

Tel: 01788 573241

Independent marriage, relationship, and family counselling and conciliation services.

Gambling

Gamblers Anonymous
PO Box 88
London
SW10 0EU

Tel: 0171 352 3060

Help advice and information for gambling addicts.

Health

Health Information Service

Tel: 0800 665544

Calls are automatically routed to nearest office for local information. Supplies up-to-date information on self-help groups and voluntary organisations.

Mental Health

The Mental Health Foundation
8 Hallam Street
London WIN 6DH
Tel: 0171 580 0145

The Mental Health Foundation provides a unique database of self-help and community support agencies both national and local throughout the UK.

MIND – National Association for Mental Health

Tel: 0181 519 2122

Retirement

Pre-retirement Association of GB and Northern Ireland
Nodus Centre
University Campus
Guildford
Surrey GU2 5RX

Tel: 01483 39323

Support and help for those who are going to retire or are retired.

Samaritans
17 Uxbridge Road
Slough
Berkshire SL1 1SN

Tel: 01753 32713

Twenty-four hour service for the suicidal and despairing. The telephone number of your local branch will be in the telephone book.

Smoking

ASH (Action on Smoking and Health)
5–11 Mortimer Street
London W1N 7RH

Tel: 0171 637 9843

Advice and help for smokers who want to give up.

Women's Health

Women's Health
52–54 Featherstone Street
London EC1Y 8RT

Tel: 0171 251 6580

Will provide details of local support groups. Reference library available for personal callers.

Appendix 2(a)

CODE OF ETHICS AND PRACTICE FOR COUNSELLORS (1993)

The BAC regularly updates its codes of practice; copies and further information can be obtained from BAC on 01788 550899.

1.   Status of this code

1.1   In response to the experience of members of BAC, this code is a revision of the 1992 code.

2.   Introduction

2.1   The purpose of this code is to establish and maintain standards for counsellors who are members of BAC, and to inform and protect members of the public seeking and using their services.

2.2   All members of this Association are required to abide by existing codes appropriate to them. They thereby accept a common frame of reference within which to manage their responsibilities to clients, colleagues, members of this Association and the wider community. Whilst this code cannot resolve all ethical and practice related issues, it aims to provide a framework for addressing ethical issues and to encourage optimum levels of practice. Counsellors will need to judge which parts of this code apply to particular situations. They may have to decide between conflicting responsibilities.

2.3   This Association has a Complaints Procedure which

can lead to the expulsion of members for breaches of its Codes of Ethics & Practice.

3.   The Nature of Counselling

3.1   The overall aim of counselling is to provide an opportunity for the client to work towards living in a more satisfying and resourceful way. The term 'counselling' includes work with individuals, pairs or groups of people often, but not always, referred to as 'clients'. The objectives of particular counselling relationships will vary according to the client's needs. Counselling may be concerned with developmental issues, addressing and resolving specific problems, making decisions, coping with crisis, developing personal insight and knowledge, working through feelings of inner conflict or improving relationships with others. The counsellor's role is to facilitate the client's work in ways which respect the client's values, personal resources and capacity for self-determination.

3.2   Only when both the user and the recipient explicitly agree to enter into a counselling relationship does it become 'counselling' rather than the use of 'counselling skills'.

3.3   It is not possible to make a generally accepted distinction between counselling and psychotherapy. There are well-founded traditions which use the terms interchangeably and others which distinguish them. Regardless of the theoretical approaches preferred by individual counsellors, there are ethical issues which are common to all counselling situations.

4.   The Structure of this Code

This code has been divided into two parts. The Code

of Ethics outlines the fundamental values of counselling and a number of general principles arising from these. The Code of Practice applies these principles to the counselling situation.

A.   CODE OF ETHICS

A.1   Counselling is a non-exploitative activity. Its basic values are integrity, impartiality, and respect. Counsellors should take the same degree of care to work ethically whether the counselling is paid or voluntary.

A.2   Client Safety:
All reasonable steps should be taken to ensure the client's safety during counselling.

A.3   Clear Contracts:
The terms on which counselling is being offered should be made clear to clients before counselling commences. Subsequent revisions of these terms should be agreed in advance of any change.

A.4   Competence:
Counsellors shall take all reasonable steps to monitor and develop their own competence and to work within the limits of that competence. This includes having appropriate and ongoing counselling supervision/consultative support.

B.   CODE OF PRACTICE

B.1   Introduction:
This code applies these values and ethical principles to more specific situations which may arise in the practice of counselling.

B.2   Issues of Responsibility:
B.2.1   The counsellor–client relationship is the foremost

ethical concern, but it does not exist in social isolation. For this reason, the counsellor's responsibilities to the client, to themselves, colleagues, other members of the Association and members of the wider community are listed under separate headings.

B.2.2   To the Client:
Client Safety

2.2.1   Counsellors should take all reasonable steps to ensure that the client suffers neither physical nor psychological harm during counselling.

2.2.2   Counsellors do not normally give advice.

Client Autonomy

2.2.3   Counsellors are responsible for working in ways which promote the client's control over his/her own life, and respects the client's ability to make decisions and change in the light of his/her own beliefs and values.

2.2.4   Counsellors do not normally act on behalf of their clients. If they do, it will be only at the express request of the client, or else in the exceptional circumstances detailed in B.4.

2.2.5   Counsellors are responsible for setting and monitoring boundaries between the counselling relationship and any other kind of relationship, and making this explicit to the client.

2.2.6   Counsellors must not exploit their clients financially, sexually, emotionally, or in any other way. Engaging in sexual activity with the client is unethical.

2.2.7   Clients should be offered privacy for counselling sessions. The client should not be observed by anyone other than their counsellor(s) without having given his/her informed consent. This also applies to audio/video taping of counselling sessions.

Pre-Counselling Information

2.2.8   Any publicity material and all written and oral information should reflect accurately the nature of the service on offer, and the training, qualifications and relevant experience of the counsellor (see also B.6).

2.2.9   Counsellors should take all reasonable steps to honour undertakings offered in their pre-counselling information.

Contracting

2.2.10   Clear contracting enhances and shows respect for the client's autonomy.

2.2.11   Counsellors are responsible for communicating the terms on which counselling is being offered, including availability, the degree of confidentiality offered, and their expectations of clients regarding fees, cancelled appointments and any other significant matters. The communication of terms and any negotiations over these should be concluded before the client incurs any financial liability.

2.2.12   It is the client's choice whether or not to participate in counselling. Reasonable steps should be taken in the course of the counselling relationship to ensure that the client is given an opportunity to review the terms on which counselling is being offered and the methods of counselling being used.

2.2.13   Counsellors should avoid unnecessary conflicts of interest and are expected to make explicit to the client any relevant conflicts of interest.

2.2.14   If records of counselling sessions are kept, clients should be made aware of this. At the client's request information should be given about access to these records, their availability to other people, and the degree of security with which they are kept (see B.4).

2.2.15   Counsellors have a responsibility to establish with clients what other therapeutic or helping relationships are current. Counsellors should gain the client's permission before conferring with other professional workers.

2.2.16   Counsellors should be aware that computer-based records are subject to statutory regulations under the Data Protection Act 1984. From time to time the government introduces changes in the regulations concerning the client's right of access to his/her own records. Current regulations have implications for counsellors working in social service and health care settings.

Counsellor Competence

2.2.17   Counsellors should monitor actively the limitations of their own competence through counselling supervision/consultative support, and by seeking the views of their clients and other counsellors. Counsellors should work within their own known limits.

2.2.18   Counsellors should not counsel when their functioning is impaired due to personal or emotional difficulties, illness, disability, alcohol, drugs or for any other reason.

2.2.19   It is an indication of the competence of counsellors when they recognise their inability to counsel a client or clients and make appropriate referrals.

B.2.3   To Former Clients:

2.3.1   Counsellors remain accountable for relationships with former clients and must exercise caution over entering into friendships, business relationships, sexual relationships, training and other relationships. Any changes in relationship must be discussed in counselling supervision. The decision about any change(s) in relationship with former clients should take into account whether the issues and power dynamics present during the counselling relationship have been resolved and properly ended.

2.3.2   Counsellors who belong to organisations which prohibit sex with all former clients are bound by that commitment.

B.2.4   To Self as Counsellor:

2.4.1   Counsellors have a responsibility to themselves and their clients to maintain their own effectiveness, resilience and ability to help clients. They are expected to monitor their own personal functioning and to seek help and/or withdraw from counselling, whether temporarily or permanently, when their personal resources are sufficiently depleted to require this (see also B.3).

2.2.2   Counsellors should have received adequate basic training before commencing counselling, and should maintain ongoing professional development.

2.4.3 Counsellors are encouraged to review periodically their need for professional indemnity insurance and to take out such a policy when appropriate.

2.4.4 Counsellors should take all reasonable steps to ensure their own physical safety.

B.2.5 To other Counsellors:

2.5.1 Counsellors should not conduct themselves in their counselling-related activities in ways which undermine public confidence in either their role as a counsellor or in the work of other counsellors.

2.5.2 If a counsellor suspects misconduct by another counsellor which cannot be resolved or remedied after discussion with the counsellor concerned, they should implement the Complaints Procedure, doing so without breaches of confidentiality other than those necessary for investigating the complaint (see B.9).

B.2.6 To Colleagues and Members of the Caring Professions:

2.6.1 Counsellors should be accountable for their services to colleagues, employers and funding bodies as appropriate. The means of achieving this should be consistent with respecting the needs of the client outlined in B.2.2.7, B.2.2.13 and B.4.

2.6.2 Counsellors are encouraged to increase their colleagues' understanding of the counselling role. No colleague or significant member of the caring professions should be led to believe that a service is being offered by the counsellor which is not, as this may deprive the client of the offer of such a service from elsewhere.

2.6.3 Counsellors should accept their part in exploring and resolving conflicts of interest between themselves and their agencies, especially where this has implications for the client (see also B.2.2.13).

B.2.7 To the Wider Community:
Law

2.7.1 Counsellors should work within the law.

2.7.2   Counsellors should take all reasonable steps to be aware of current law affecting the work of the counsellor. A counsellor's ignorance of the law is no defence against legal liability or penalty including inciting or 'counselling', which has a specific legal sense, the commission of offences by clients.

Social Context

2.7.3   Counsellors will take all reasonable steps to take account of the client's social context.

B.3   Counselling Supervision/Consultative Support:

B.3.1   It is a breach of the ethical requirement for counsellors to practise without regular counselling supervision/consultative support.

B.3.2   Counselling supervision/consultative support refers to a formal arrangement which enables counsellors to discuss their counselling regularly with one or more people who have an understanding of counselling and counselling supervision/consultative support. Its purpose is to ensure the efficacy of the counsellor–client relationship. It is a confidential relationship (see also B.4).

B.3.3   Counsellors who have line managers owe them appropriate managerial accountability for their work. The counselling supervisor role should be independent of the line manager role. However, where the counselling supervisor is also the line manager, the counsellor should also have access to independent consultative support.

B.3.4   The volume of supervision should be in proportion to the volume of counselling work undertaken and the experience of the counsellor.

B.3.5   Whenever possible, the discussion of cases within supervision/consultative support should take place without revealing the personal identity of the client.

B.3.6   The ethics and practice of counselling supervision/ consultative support are outlined further in their own specific code: the Code of Ethics & Practice for the Supervision of Counsellors (see also B.9).

B.4   **Confidentiality: Clients, Colleagues and Others:**

B.4.1   Confidentiality is a means of providing the client with safety and privacy. For this reason any limitation on the degree of confidentiality offered is likely to diminish the usefulness of counselling.

B.4.2   Counsellors treat with confidence personal information about clients, whether obtained directly or indirectly or by inference. Such information includes name, address, biographical details, and other descriptions of the client's life and circumstances which might result in identification of the client.

B.4.3   Counsellors should work within the current agreement with their client about confidentiality.

B.4.4   Exceptional circumstances may arise which give the counsellor good grounds for believing that the client will cause serious physical harm to others or themselves, or have harm caused to him/her. In such circumstances the client's consent to a change in the agreement about confidentiality should be sought whenever possible unless there are also good grounds for believing the client is no longer able to take responsibility for his/her own actions. Whenever possible, the decision to break confidentiality agreed between a counsellor and client should be made only after consultation with a counselling supervisor or an experienced counsellor.

B.4.5   Any breaking of confidentiality should be minimised both by restricting the information conveyed to that which is pertinent to the immediate situation and to those persons who can provide the help required by the client. The ethical considerations involve balancing between acting in the best interests of the client and in ways which enable clients to resume taking responsibility for their actions, a very high priority for counsellors, and the counsellor's responsibilities to the wider community (see B.2.7 and B.4.4).

B.4.6   Counsellors should take all reasonable steps to communicate clearly the extent of the confidentiality they are offering to clients. This should normally be made clear in the pre-counselling information or initial contracting.

B.4.7   If counsellors include consultations with colleagues and others within the confidential relationship, this should be stated to the client at the beginning of counselling.

B.4.8   Care must be taken to ensure that personally identifiable information is not transmitted through overlapping networks of confidential relationships. For this reason, it is good practice to avoid identifying specific clients during counselling supervision/consultative support and other consultations unless there are sound reasons for doing so (see also B.2.2.14 and B.4.2).

B.4.9   Any agreement between the counsellor and client about confidentiality may be reviewed and changed by joint negotiations.

B.4.10   Agreements about confidentiality continue after the client's death unless there are overriding legal or ethical considerations.

B.4.11   Counsellors hold different views about whether or not a client expressing serious suicidal intentions forms sufficient grounds for breaking confidentiality. Counsellors should consider their own views and practice and communicate them to clients and any significant others where appropriate (see also B.2.6.2).

B.4.12   Special care is required when writing about specific counselling situations for case studies, reports or publication. It is important that the author either has the client's informed consent, or effectively disguises the client's identity.

B.4.13   Any discussion between the counsellor and others should be purposeful and not trivialising.

B.5   **Confidentiality in the Legal Process:**

B.5.1   Generally speaking there is no legal duty to give information spontaneously or on request until instructed to do so by a court. Refusal to answer police questions is not an offence, although lying could be. In general terms, the only circumstances in which the police can require an answer about a client, and when refusal to answer would be an offence, relate to the prevention of terrorism. It is good practice to ask police personnel to clarify their legal right to an answer before refusing to give one.

B.5.2   Withholding information about a crime that one knows has been committed or is about to be committed is not an offence, save exceptionally. Anyone hearing of terrorist activities should immediately take legal advice.

B.5.3   There is no legal obligation to answer a solicitor's enquiry or to make a statement for the purpose of legal proceedings, unless ordered to do so by a court.

B.5.4   There is no legal obligation to attend court at the request of parties involved in a case, or at the request of their lawyers, until a witness summons or subpoena is issued to require attendance to answer questions or produce documents.

B.5.5   Once in the witness box, there is a duty to answer questions when instructed to do so by the court. Refusal to answer could be punished as contempt of court unless there are legal grounds for not doing so. (It has been held that communications between the counsellor and client during an attempt at 'reconciliation' in matrimonial cases are privileged and thus do not require disclosure unless the client waives this privilege. This does not seem to apply to other kinds of cases.)

B.5.6   The police have powers to seize confidential files if they have obtained a warrant from a circuit judge. Obstructing the police from taking them in these circumstances may be an offence.

B.5.7   Counsellors should seek legal advice and/or contact this Association if they are in any doubt about their legal rights and obligations before acting in ways which conflict with their agreement with clients who are directly affected (see also B.2.7.1).

B.6   Advertising/Public Statements:
B.6.1   When announcing counselling services, counsellors should limit the information to name, relevant qualifications, address, telephone number, hours available, and a brief listing of the services offered.

B.6.2   All such announcements should be accurate in every particular.

B.6.3   Counsellors should distinguish between membership of this Association and accredited practitioner status in their public statements. In particular, the former should not be used to imply the latter.

B.6.4   Counsellors should not display an affiliation with an organisation in a manner which falsely implies the sponsorship or verification of that organisation.

B.7   Research:
B.7.1   The use of personally identifiable material gained from clients or by the observation of counselling

should be used only after the client has given consent, usually in writing, and care has been taken to ensure that consent was given freely.

B.7.2 Counsellors conducting research should use their data accurately and restrict their conclusions to those compatible with their methodology.

B.8 Resolving Conflicts between Ethical Priorities:

B.8.1 Counsellors will, from time to time, find themselves caught between conflicting ethical principles. In these circumstances, they are urged to consider the particular situation in which they find themselves and to discuss the situation with their counselling supervisor and/or other experienced counsellors. Even after conscientious consideration of the salient issues, some ethical dilemmas cannot be resolved easily or wholly satisfactorily.

B.8.2 Ethical issues may arise which have not yet been given full consideration. The Standards & Ethics Sub-Committee of this Association is interested in hearing of the ethical difficulties of counsellors, as this helps to inform discussion regarding good practice.

B.9 The Availability of other Codes and Guidelines Relating to Counselling:

B.9.1 The following codes and procedures have been passed by the Annual General Meetings of the British Association for Counselling:

Code of Ethics & Practice for Counselling Skills applies to members who would not regard themselves as counsellors, but who use counselling skills to support other roles.
Code of Ethics & Practice for the Supervision of Counsellors exists to guide members offering supervision to counsellors and to help counsellors seeking supervision.
Code of Ethics & Practice for Trainers exists to guide

members offering training to counsellors and to help members of the public seeking counselling training. *Complaints Procedure* exists to guide members of BAC and their clients resolving complaints about breaches of the Codes of Ethics & Practice.

Copies and other guidelines and information sheets relevant to maintaining ethical standards of practice can be obtained from the BAC office, 1 Regent Place, Rugby CV21 2PJ.

Guidelines also available:
Telephone Helplines: Guidelines for Good Practice is intended to establish standards for people working on telephone helplines (sponsored by British Telecom). Single copies available from BSS, PO Box 7, London W3 6XJ.

Appendix 2(b)

CODE OF ETHICS AND PRACTICE FOR COUNSELLING SKILLS (1989)

A.   Introduction

The purpose of this Code is:
☐ to clarify the ethical issues for anyone using counselling skills
☐ to establish standards of practice
☐ to inform members of the public about their use.

One of the purposes of Codes of Practice is to clarify the expectations of both providers and users of services.

B.   The Meaning of Counselling Skills

1.1   The term 'counselling skills' does not have a single definition which is universally accepted. For the purpose of this code, 'counselling skills' are distinguished from 'listening skills' and from 'counselling'. Although the distinction is not always a clear one, because the term 'counselling skills' contains elements of these other two activities, it has its own place in the continuum between them. What distinguishes the use of counselling skills from these other two activities are the intentions of the user, which is to enhance the performance of their functional role, as line manager, nurse, tutor, social worker, personnel officer, voluntary worker, etc., the recipient will, in turn, perceive them in that role.

1.2   Ask yourself the following questions:
a) Are you using counselling skills to enhance your

communication with someone but without taking on the role of their counsellor?

b) Does the recipient perceive you as acting within your professional/caring role (which is NOT that of being their counsellor)?

i.   If the answer is YES to both these questions, you are using counselling skills in your functional role and should use this document.

ii. If the answer is NO to both, you are counselling and should look to the Code of Ethics & Practice for Counsellors for guidance.

iii. If the answer is YES to one and NO to the other, you have a conflict of expectations and should resolve it.

Only when both the user and the recipient explicitly contract to enter into a counselling relationship does it cease to be 'using counselling skills' and become 'counselling'. When this occurs, the Code of Ethics & Practice for Counsellors should be referred to.

C.   THE CODE OF ETHICS

C.1   Issues of Responsibility

1.1   The users of counselling skills are responsible for the appropriate use of those skills within any existing Code of Ethics & Practice governing their functional roles. If there is no existing Code of Ethics & Practice then the user's Agency or occupation may find it helpful to reflect on such issues.

1.2   It is desirable that anyone in receipt of services which include the use of counselling skills should have access to the Code of Ethics & Practice governing their use.

C.2   Issues of Competence

2.1   The user of counselling skills should ensure that s/he has received sufficient training to be able to use them appropriately.

2.2   Training in counselling skills is not sufficient for users to consider themselves qualified counsellors.

2.3   The user of counselling skills should maintain his/her level of competence.

D.   THE CODE OF PRACTICE

D.1   Management of the Work

1.1   The user of counselling skills is responsible for their use in a way which is consistent with good practice in the user's functional role.

1.2   The user should be clear whose interests s/he is serving. This may involve discussion of any conflict of interests.

1.3   Counselling skills should be used in accordance with the Codes of Ethics & Practice governing the user's functional role.

D.2   Confidentiality

2.1   While there may be no automatic presumption that the relationship between the user and the recipient of counselling skills is confidential, nonetheless the user should work within D2.2 – D2.4.

2.2   The user of counselling skills should work within any agreement made with the recipient about confidentiality.

2.3   Any agreement made between the user and the recipient should be consistent with any written Code(s) governing the functional role of the user of counselling skills.

2.4   Exceptional circumstances in which the user of counselling skills might break her/his agreement about confidentiality with the recipient should be indicated within any written Code. The user should indicate this at the time of making the agreement. The exact circumstances in which any agreement about confidentiality may be broken should be included within any written Code.

D.3   Endorsements of Codes of Practice

3.1   Individual and Organisational members of the British Association for Counselling may submit Draft Codes of Ethics & Practice to:
The Convenor, Standards & Ethics Sub-Committee, British Association for Counselling, 37a Sheep Street, Rugby, Warwickshire CV21 3BX, for constructive comments.

3.2   Codes which have been approved by the Standards & Ethics Sub-Committee of this Association may contain a statement to this effect.

ADDENDUM

The following Codes of Practice may be useful:
Existing Codes of Ethics & Practice for;
    Counsellors
Trainers
    Supervision of Counsellors
Guidelines for Good Practice for Telephone Helplines
Counselling in General Practice: Guides for GPs and
    Counsellors.

Appendix 2(c)

CODE OF ETHICS AND PRACTICE FOR TRAINERS (1985)

A.   CODE OF ETHICS

Introduction

The purpose of this Code of Ethics is to establish and maintain standards for trainers and to inform and protect members of the public seeking counselling training.

This document should be seen in relation to the Code of Ethics and Practice for Counsellors.

Ethical standards comprise such values as integrity, competence, confidentiality and responsibility. Members of this Association, in assenting to this Code, accept their responsibilities to trainees, colleagues and clients, this Association, their agencies and society.

Trainers are those who train people to become counsellors or who train people in counselling skills.

Trainers endeavour to ensure that when trainees complete the programme of training, the trainees are competent to serve the best interest of the client.

The relationship between trainers and trainees is similar in some respects to that between counsellors and clients. Trainees, during some of this training, may find themselves in a vulnerable situation with regard to a trainer where painful and potentially damaging material may be revealed which needs to be handled in a sensitive and caring manner. In other respects, the relationship is different. Trainees are adult learners who bring to the training their prior experience and personal style. This should be respected by trainers and only challenged in relation to the stated objectives of the particular training.

Trainers need to be guided by this ethical code so that they can maintain the highest standards of responsibility towards trainees. Therefore this Code of Ethics is a framework within which to work – more a set of instruments than a set of instructions.

1. **Issues of Responsibility**
2. **Issues of Competence**

1.   Issues of Responsibility

1.1.   Training a person as a counsellor in counselling skills is a deliberately undertaken responsibility.

1.2.   Trainers are responsible for the observance of the principles embodied in this Code of Ethics and Practice for Trainers and the Code of Ethics for Counsellors.

1.3.   Trainers must recognise the value and dignity of trainees irrespective of origin, status, sex, sexual orientation, age, belief or contribution to society.

1.4.   Trainers accept a responsibility to encourage and facilitate the self-development of trainees whilst also establishing clear working agreements which indicate the responsibility of trainees for their own continued learning and self-monitoring.

1.5.   Trainers are responsible for setting and monitoring the boundaries between working relationships, and friendships or other relationships and for making boundaries between therapy, consultancy, supervision and training explicit to trainees.

1.6.   Trainers are responsible for ensuring that the satisfaction of their own emotional needs is not dependent upon relationships with their trainees.

1.7.   Trainers should not engage in sexual activity with their trainees whilst also engaging in a training relationship.

1.8.   Trainers should not accept their own trainees for treatment or individual therapy for personal or sexual difficulties should these arise or be revealed during the programme of training. Trainees should be referred to an appropriate individual or agency.

2.   Issues of Competence

2.1.   Trainers, having undertaken a basic course in counselling training, should commit themselves to undertake further training as trainers at regular intervals thereafter and consistently seek ways of increasing their professional development and self-awareness.

2.2.   Trainers must monitor their training work and be able to account to trainees and colleagues for what they do and why.

2.3.   Trainers should monitor the limits of their competence.

2.4.   Trainers have a responsibility to themselves and to their trainees to maintain their own effectiveness, resilience, and ability to help trainees, and to know when their personal resources are so depleted as to make it necessary for them to seek help and/or withdraw from counselling training whether temporarily or permanently.

B.   CODE OF PRACTICE

Introduction

This Code of Practice is intended to provide more specific information and guidance regarding the implementation of the principles embodied in the Code of Ethics for Trainers.

1.   Management of the Training Work

1.1.   Trainers should inform trainees as appropriate about their own training, philosophy and theoretical approach, qualifications, and the methods they use.

1.2.   Trainers should be explicit regarding the training programmes and courses offered and what is involved. It is desirable that there should be some consistency between the theoretical orientation of the course and the teaching methods used on it, eg client-centred courses will tend to be trainee-centred.

1.3.   Any fees required should be disclosed before courses begin.

1.4.   Trainers should be open with intending trainees regarding potential suitability for training and make clear what selection procedures are involved.

1.5.   Trainers have a responsibility to confirm with trainees what therapeutic or helping relationships are in existence before the course begins, and enable trainees to consider their own needs for personal therapy outside the course and the contribution it might make to their work during their training programme.

1.6.   Trainers should ensure that practical experience of counselling under regular supervision should be part of counselling training.

1.7.   Trainers should arrange for initial, continuous, and final assessments of trainees' work and their continuing fitness for the course. Trainers should make trainees aware of this process.

1.8.   Trainers should provide opportunities for trainees to work with self individually, and in groups, so that trainees may learn to integrate professional practice and personal insights.

1.9.   Trainers should ensure that trainees are given the opportunity to discuss their experience of the course in groups, individually or both.

1.10.   Trainers should encourage self-assessment and peer assessment amongst their trainees.

1.11.   Trainees are to ensure that their trainees are made aware of the distinctions between counselling, managerial, and consultancy tasks and roles in training and supervision.

1.12.   Trainers who become aware of a conflict between their obligation to a trainee and their obligation to an agency or organisation employing them will make explicit to the trainee the nature of the loyalties involved.

1.13.   Where personal differences cannot be resolved the trainer will consult with and where appropriate refer to another colleague.

1.14.   Trainers should arrange for regular evaluation and assessment of their work by a professional supervisor or consultant and should ask for full and prompt information of the results.

1.15.   Trainers should take account of the limitations of their competence and make appropriate arrangements when necessary.

2.   Confidentiality

2.1.   Confidentiality must be maintained with regard to information of a personal or sexual nature obtained by the trainer.

2.2.   Trainers may not reveal confidential information concerning trainees to any other person or through any public medium except to those to whom trainers owe accountability for training work (in the case of those working within an agency or organisational setting) or on whom trainers rely for support and supervision.

2.3.   Confidentiality does not preclude the disclosure of confidential information relating to trainees when relevant to the following:
a) evaluation of the trainee by trainers or training committee
b) recommendations concerning trainees for professional purposes
c) pursuit of disciplinary action involving trainees in matters pertaining to ethical standards
d) selection procedures.

2.4.   Information about specific trainees may only be used for publication in appropriate journals or meetings with the trainee's permission and with anonymity preserved when the trainee so specifies.

2.5.   Discussion by trainees of their trainees with professional colleagues should be purposeful and not trivialising.

British Association
for Counselling
1 Regent Place
Rugby CV21 2PJ
Tel: 01788 578328
Fax: 01788 562189

INDEX